WAL
LIGHT
WITH ME

A Journey of Self-Discovery,
Healing and In-Lightenment

SHAWNEE RENÉE BENTON

Walk in the Light with Me:

A Journey of Self-Discovery, Healing and In-lightenment

Cover Design and Editing: Robin Devonish Scott,
The Self-Publishing Maven

ISBN-13: 978-0692337837

ISBN-10: 0692337830

Printed in the United States of America

www.thegriotshealingcircle.com

www.sowleadership.com

TABLE OF CONTENTS

ACKNOWLEDGMENTS

This book is dedicated to my two mothers; Jill who birthed me and Joyce who raised me, and all of my extended family members to whom I owe my life. I give thanks and acknowledge each of you for being the resilient, powerful and creative people that you are. Your stories and your histories have influenced and inspired mine. I trust that we will spend the rest of our time on the planet, building and sharing in the service of our individual and collective dreams and the fulfillment of our destinies. I also salute and give honor to my ancestors who are protecting and guiding me in the spirit realm: my father Kenneth Morgan, grandfathers John Morgan and James Benton, my great-grandfather Walter Dixon, my grandmother Ruth Morgan, my great grandmother Margaret, my great-great grandmother Strellis, my aunt Thomasina, my uncle Christopher, my brother Michael and all of the souls that are part of my lineage whose names I do not know.

To my children Shamony, Jasmine and Najiah-Sekou: you are the spark of light that glimmers in the distance when I have lost my way. Each of your births was the catalyst for a major shift in my life and allowed me to see my own reflection, even when I didn't want to. You have motivated me to do deep and transformative work on myself. I thank you for your patience, your candor, your love, your wonderful sense of humor, and the light energy that you've brought to my life during times when I wanted to dwell in the darkness. You ***inner***-stand me and I am grateful.

To all of the teachers, mentors, friends and colleagues who are too numerous to name, I thank you. To the powerful sisters who have befriended, mentored and nurtured me as I've moved through the various phases and stages of my life: Janine, Letia, Janet, Kim, Jennifer, Monica, Joyce, Robin, Laura and Erica, I thank you. To the brothers who have shown me love, extended their hands and their hearts, helped me to balance my masculine and feminine energies and heal from my hurts: Daymion, Alex, Sean, Lesley, Fred, Mike, Brian, Darryl and Diego, I thank you.

To the spiritual teachers and advisors who recognized my gifts, shared their energy, knowledge and wisdom with me and who lovingly and patiently helped me move forward on my spiritual path: Rev. John Mason, Rev. Walter A. Jones, Rev. Tinsdale, Rev. Johnny Ray Youngblood, Rev. Lesley F. Shannon, Baba Obediah Wright, Jesse Wooden Jr., Sehu, Jennifer, Shakuwra, Osunyoyin, the late Heather Vaughn, who is now supporting me from heaven AND my higher self who whispers to me every day, I thank you.

To the people and communities who have fueled my creative genius, expanded my skills, provided me with the tools to stand in my greatness and helped me to amplify my voice and my reach: St. Paul Community Baptist Church, Mt. Pisgah Baptist Church, Hudson Valley Psychodrama Institute, Big Apple Playback Theater and Landmark Worldwide, I thank you.

And finally, to the Creator of all life and the vast network of guides, angels and ancestors who walk with, cover and speak to me through my five senses and my third eye, I thank you. Your messages are clear, your energy is felt, and your support is a blessing too expansive to express in words.

INTRODUCTION

What an awesome gift we have been bestowed by the Creator: to live everyday of our lives with the ability to *choose*. As part of our human experience, we are provided pathways, entrances and exits that can illuminate the way for our true calling on this earthly plane or allow us to remain in a state of perpetual darkness. Whatever the decision, Beloved, there is much to celebrate and be thankful for. For we are spiritual beings having an earthly experience and from these sacred positions, we possess all of the power and ingredients to contemplate, envision and make manifest our wildest, most extravagant dreams.

Your possession of this book is an example of your spirit speaking to your Divine mind and a sign of you awakening to something greater than yourself. The questions that may be welling up inside of you as you hold this tool of transformation and enlightenment may be "Who am I and how will this apply to me?" Well, Beloved, the answer that Spirit is presenting to you in this *right now* moment is, "You *are* what you *are,* and that is enough." You have taken this step and chosen this book because YOU are both the question and the answer. There is a mystery and complexity to your existence as well as a simplicity to it that can no longer remain hidden or denied.

There is much to be learned while we are here in these bodies and even more to be absorbed before we make our transition back into the spirit realm. Time, and our perception of it, has greatly impacted our journey and our mishandling and misinterpretation of it has had a profound impact on our healing and growth. We can either dwell in time as prisoners of it or we can utilize its power to shift, transform and create things. Beloved, we have the power to choose that which will restore and replenish us. We are not creatures floating aimlessly and powerlessly on the periphery as the world moves before us. We are active participants with the ability to write, rewrite or even erase the script of the lives we've chosen to live. Beloved, today, as you turn these pages and embark on this journey of higher learning, revelation and discovery, I ask that you allow yourself to tap into your creative and co-creative energies so that you may produce the outcomes that you envision for yourself and those you love.

As you read this book, think about the goals, desires and dreams that live in your spirit and call them to the forefront so that this power source, this resource for elevated living, can support and energize them. You will not be alone in this process unless you choose to be. Yours is not an isolated walk or journey; for with every step, your existence and your actions are being impacted by something or someone outside of you. As you read and connect with the words, concepts and activities laid out in each of the pages of this book, please know that you are being carried ever so gently into a space of higher awareness; an elevated space where you can see, hear and feel things from a heightened state of being. If you trust the process and surrender to it, you can, and will, feel a shift within your core; a shift that will be palpable to others; a shift that will expose you to the greatness that you were born to be.

THE WORD

Since I was a little girl, I have had a deep and intimate relationship with *words*. I was a precocious child who started talking, reading and writing at an early age. Words, and everything associated with them, were my world and as I gained mastery over them, it was only natural for me to enhance the relationship by adding singing and acting to my repertoire of *word magic*. I spent hours reading books, creating and writing stories and then acting them out; either by myself or with others. I also had an obsession with television. I was so enamored with the creatures that dwelled in the box, that I would watch my favorite shows, movies and commercials until the Star-Spangled Banner played and the stations stopped broadcasting.

It was my romance with television that added to my love for stories and served as the fertilizer for the characters and scenes that emerged from my own head. My imagination was the gateway to new worlds and wonders, and provided me with an escape from the unpredictability of the "real" world and all of its accompanying emotions.

As far back as I can remember, my words have been able to move and impact people and situations. My intellect, discernment and insights were often celebrated by family and friends and sometimes criticized and ridiculed when I rubbed people the wrong way. The adults and older children in my family and community were sometimes caught off guard by the things that came up and out of me. I had adult thoughts, used adult expressions and shared adult wisdom. I questioned and challenged people and situations no matter how old they were or what was going on. I simply said what came to my mind and my heart and there were times when the persons on the receiving end of my inquiries and opinions felt that I was disrespectful, insensitive or even obnoxious. I can only recall one period in my life when my words ceased to be my refuge and I stopped speaking unless I was angry. It was a dark time in my life; the time between my pre-adolescent years and my early teens. Those who were close to me may have believed it was hormonal or depression; some didn't care because they were grateful for the quiet. Whatever the reason, it was a time in my life when I didn't have enough energy to generate the words that I loved so well. I felt an unwavering heaviness that I could not, or would not, articulate.

THE STORY

I have chosen to open this book by talking about my use of "word magic" because it provides a powerful background for the foreground of the life that I am currently living. It also allows you, the reader, to gain a greater understanding of the power that our words wield as we seek to release and restore balance in our lives. My relationship with words is tied to everything that has manifested in my life thus far; both the dark things and the things that glow.

My respect for the sharing of stories, in all forms, has fueled my work as a healer, a counselor, an advocate, a performer, a spiritual advisor, a guide, a mother and a friend. It has moved people to entrust me with their most precious secrets and to share their lives with me in ways that I, and they, would have never imagined. It has opened doors for me in every aspect of my life and has closed some as well.

I must confess that I have spent the bulk of my life in a state of oblivion about the power of words. For more years than I care to admit, I was unaware that my ability to "express" and "declare" was a gift. In fact, I spent most of my life speaking and sharing with others without balance, structure, rhyme or reason. Depending on the person and the situation, my stories would seep or leap out of me, unfiltered and unsolicited. They would land on the heads and the hearts of each unsuspecting target and leave an indelible mark on them and the relationship. For many, my story or truth-telling was unnerving, disruptive, overwhelming and anxiety-provoking.

For others, my willingness to share my stories provided an opening for attacks or an opportunity for manipulation. Just a few years shy of my fortieth birthday, the mystery and magic of words were revealed to me, and a profound and pronounced shift in power and perspective ensued. Since that awakening, I have gained mastery over the use of story as a tool for healing and transformation and I have come to learn that the ritual of "telling" is intimately tied to spiritual expansion and the unveiling of one's destiny. This, Beloved, is the reason why you are reading this book today.

When I was finally able to hear and obey the whispers—and sometimes, shouts—from the Creator, my purpose and position on this earth was revealed. I discovered that I was called to be a *Griot or storyteller*; an ancient, sacred and celebrated position where the holder of the title is required to be a repository for the stories of his/her people; an orator, lyricist, musician and counselor. At first, there was incredible resistance to the fullness of the role. I started thinking about the meaning and the magnitude of such a position and what it would take for me to step into that energy and to claim and wear that power. I recognized that the role and responsibilities of a *Griot* was not for the faint of heart and I wasn't sure if I was built for such a role. Being the excavator and holder of the heart stories that live inside of people takes great courage, flexibility, wisdom and compassion and I questioned whether I had or could be those things. The thought of standing before an individual, a family, a community, a nation to present its history, sing its heart songs, and share its testaments of pain and triumph scared the hell out of me. I also felt that it would require a hundred times more courage, authenticity and humility to tell my own story.

A MESSAGE FROM *THE "GRIOT"*

INspiration is the fertilizer for INvention and INnovation;

For when we are INdwelled by Spirit, we ENter a state of "beINg"

where our INtuition allows us to ENvision, INterpret, and INvest

IN the evolution of ourselves and of humanity

– Shawnee Renée

THE STORYTELLER

We are all *Griots*. We are all master storytellers and historians who possess the keys to unlock the formulas that make up our earthly existence. However, many of us have forgotten that we have this gift and have unconsciously misfiled the tools to activate it. There are a variety of reasons, all legitimate and justifiable, for our forgetting or repressing our abilities as storytellers and story keepers. Some of this forgetting is the result of conditioning or what we were taught, either overtly or covertly, by our caregivers and by society. Some of the blockage is part of our innate ability to protect ourselves against real or imagined pain and suffering. As human filters, we have the power to edit out the data that has the potential to shock or damage our psyches. Over millennia, we have become our own energetic grave diggers who bury our pain, wounds and traumas so deep that when we attempt to retrieve them, we are sometimes unable to find the burial sites.

Whether we learn from others or teach ourselves how to forget, the fact is that each of us, as we live and breathe, holds a string of interlocking stories in our hearts and our muscle memory that make up the tapestry of our lives. These stories lay in waiting for us to remember, rewind and replay them. They whisper to us when we are alone, in groups, in a deep sleep or daydreaming in the light of day. Our conscious and deliberate reactivation of the chronicles that live within us allows us to reach back across time and space to rediscover who we are and why we are here on the planet. Our willingness to go deep is the catalyst for the opening of a portal that will lead to the expansion of our hearts and the revelation of our truths.

Beloved, this book will allow you to tap into, and release, the Griot that dwells within. I am both a witness and a recipient of the riches that one can gain from adopting this formula for higher living and learning. It is a simple model; one that can be used to restore or enhance the balance, energy and power in your life. Each passage is designed similarly to the structure of the live groups, workshops, teleconferences and seminars that I facilitate as part of my healing work. As I became more enlightened and gained a greater understanding of my purpose on the planet, Spirit revealed that I should adopt and activate a specific blueprint that would guide the work and support my partners in healing as they moved through their own restorative processes.

This prescription for elevation was channeled through me by Spirit through pictures, spoken and written words, trainings, workshops, waking and sleeping dreams, waves of emotional content and energetic exchanges with my ancestors and guides. When all of the elements were being communicated to me, and through me, I was supported by the universe as I pieced together the puzzle that would become a mechanism for sharing stories of transformation. Throughout this process of receiving and deciphering, I was simultaneously initiating my own journey of enlightenment and self-discovery which led me out of the darkness and into the light that now illuminates my path.

THE FORMULA

As you embrace and execute the formula within the pages of this book, you are giving yourself permission to:

- **review** the stories that are part of your living portfolio;
- **reflect** on the origins, the patterns and the impact of these stories;
- **release** the habitual and programmed nature of your responses to the stories and;
- **restore** the internal order and power that you possess.

Beloved, this process is not exact and there are no right or wrong turns on this journey so I invite you to release the illusion of perfection as you begin to reawaken the sleeping giant within you. Utilize every twist and detour as an opportunity to gain a deeper understanding of yourself, of others and the world. The Creator's infinite power and genius provides an unlimited number of pathways in the universe that can render meaningful and sustainable results in your life. This book outlines the path or paths that worked for my life so as you embark on your own healing journey, please keep in mind and spirit, that some of the ingredients for the formula that I am sharing may not come together as harmoniously for you as they did for me. Whatever your unique pathway to enlightenment may be, the ultimate goal is that you discover it and that you allow it to reveal the characters, scenes and themes that have been informing your life, your choices and your outcomes. This inquiry and introspective walk is yours to own and create and if you choose to take it, you are guaranteed to unveil much.

Review

The journey to "the light" begins with a "***review***." A review is a retrospective glimpse or survey of one's life. It is a replay of the moments (scenes) and the players (characters) that have contributed to your "here and now" and supported the co-creation of the life that you are presently living. A review also provides an opportunity to revisit the string of choices and actions that have molded and shaped your "being." The intention of a review is not to dismantle, judge, persecute or even celebrate yourself. It is simply an exercise to re-call events, re-play actions and re-trace steps.

The personal reviews or testimonies from my life that open each of the chapters in this book contain pieces of my life story, my commentaries and my reflections about what occurred in my world; from my perspective and lens. The people and situations that are presented in the reviews are included to support you with understanding and/or identifying with a particular lesson or experience that led to my mind, body, spirit "awakening." It is also important to point out that my reflections are solely based on my interpretation of things that happened to me. They are neither right nor wrong; they are neither true nor false. They are simply the stories that emerged from the ingredients that created my world at that time; no more or no less.

A few years ago, when I started applying the **review, reflect, release, restore** formula to my own life, my reviews were just a skeleton of my experiences and were riddled with judgments against myself and others as well as loads and loads of analysis. After a season of intense mental, spiritual, physical and therapeutic work,

I experienced an "awakening" which altered the way that I saw and related to my stories and the people in them. If you choose to read on, you will experience some of the tiny threads that are part of the shaping of my life and have contributed to my slow ascent to a higher way of living and being in the world.

Beloved, before you continue, it is important for you to know that my quest for understanding and clarity about my "beingness" did not come overnight, nor did it happen as a result of my full cooperation. There were specific parts of my experience that I did not enter into consciously. In fact, Spirit knew that my rational mind had to be tricked or bypassed so that my higher self could do the work that needed to be done to restore order and truth in my life. If you choose to embark on your own quest for enlightenment and ***inner***standing, I encourage you to keep it simple by allowing your personal reviews to unfold slowly and gently. There is no need to compare your work to mine or to measure your experience against anyone else's. I invite you to simply listen to your inner voice and allow it to tell you and show you The Way.

While everyone's process and mode of learning and release is unique, I invite you to develop new spiritual and intellectual muscles by writing your reviews in a journal or notebook and/or expressing them out loud. All of these can be done privately and kept to yourself. However, sharing them with an objective, non-triggering witness or witnesses is highly recommended. It is also important that your reviews ONLY contain pictures, settings, words, emotions and sensory responses associated with a particular experience or event or a series of events as you remember them. This requires you to write or verbalize what occurred without the extra spin of analysis, evaluation and judgment. In order to accomplish this, you must apply a level of discipline that goes against the grain of what you have been taught and what has been modeled for you throughout your life. As humans, we are wired to judge and assign meaning to our experiences so that we can process, categorize and cope with them. However, you are highly encouraged to engage in the exercise of sharing "just the facts" so that you can begin building the muscle of unconditional love and acceptance of yourself and others despite the experience and without the spin.

Reflect

The next part of the formula is "**reflect.**" To reflect is to courageously look at yourself and your circumstances from an unfiltered lens. Honest, introspective reflection is revelatory as it allows you to see and experience what lies beneath the surface, what resonates within you and through you. When you refrain from covering your eyes, guarding your heart and protecting your ego, you will see your past from the position of the witness instead of the judge and jury. As you relinquish the roles of judge and jury, you decrease the propensity to shame, blame or project debilitating thoughts, beliefs and emotions unto yourself and others.

Beloved, we are all *meaning-making* machines and we have been working this ability since birth. Because of our "*natural*" tendency to interpret and label our actions and the actions of others, the reflection phase of your journey may produce artificial and anxiety-provoking results. As you transition into this phase, you will benefit from employing the use of additional spiritual tools and support, such as counseling, prayer, meditation, reading of sacred texts, energy work, rituals, eating healthy foods and/or exercising your body, to deactivate the habitual responses you have to the stories that are stored within you. As the stories from your life begin to rise to the surface and you feel overwhelmed or triggered by them, having a partnership with a competent advisor, therapist, coach, teacher or mentor will provide you with much needed support. I also recommend that you engage in activities that edify the mind, body and spirit. This will increase your receptivity, your vibration, your spiritual and physical strength, and your ability to continue moving toward the light.

The sections in this book that will provide you with tools to support you in the reflection phase come directly after each of the ten autobiographical reviews from my past. Following each review, there is a section called Light Revelation and then a topic or message is shared that coincides with the issue, obstacle, condition or state of mind that is presented in the review. The 10 messages that are presented in this section are a string of connecting elements which provide food for thought, identify patterns, and act as a vehicle for connection so that you may come to recognize that our stories are universal experiences. We are never alone. Our stories are part of a repetitive cycle created by the thoughts and beliefs that mankind has projected out into the ether for eons. As we engage in activities that promote and support reflection, we are able to rub off the sleep from our spiritual eyes so that the lids begin to open and our pupils dilate.

Release

The third phase of the formula is "***release.***" To release is to purge from your system the parts of your stories, memories and patterns that have supported the development of a life script that may be hindering or blocking you from functioning from the highest vibration possible. We've all been programmed, by ourselves and others, to think, be and act a particular way. When we encounter specific situations, especially those that remind us of experiences from the past, we unconsciously tap into our historical data bank to activate a learned response. Many of our responses are on automatic pilot and we regurgitate the lines, act out the staging, and reach for the props that we are accustomed to using. This may or may not be serving us on our journeys, however, these words, actions and interactions have created an illusion of safety and so we depend on them.

Beloved, it requires a certain level of awareness and self-reflection to recognize that we are living in, and responding to, a dream of our own creation. As depicted in the movie The Matrix, when we unplug from the façade that we have designed and constructed, and we awaken from this hallucination we call life, we are afforded an opportunity to cut and rewire the program, or risk being pulled back into a state of un-consciousness where our higher voices are either muted or shut off. For some, unconscious and mundane living is a preferred state of being because it is what they are most familiar with. For others, this dream state has become a perpetual nightmare and their spirits are fighting to wake up. Whether the choice is to wake up or remain asleep, we are all entitled to make it and maintain it.

Once again, the 10 messages in each chapter, as well as the sections entitled Lessons from the Light and Visions of Illumination, have been included in this book to support you in releasing the scripts and patterns that exist in your life. My own awakening required that I engage in rituals and sacred rites to break through the protective shields and deconstruct the walls of the fortress that I had built around my mind, heart and spirit. These actions realigned me with the light that was buried deep within and helped me to release some of the patterns and cycles that I had repeated again and again over the course of my life.

Beloved, whether you are aware of it or not, you are energetically, psychologically, physically, mentally and emotionally attached to your patterns. One of the challenges of release is that not all of your patterns and conditioning have hurt you. Some have served as the catalyst for major movement and successes in your life. Some of your programming have been a shield of defense against real and perceived hurt or harm and have literally and figuratively saved your life. As you read, relate and respond to the contents of this book, I invite you to *inner*-stand that there is nothing broken or incomplete within you. These writings are an offering and an invitation. They provide you with a mechanism to raise your awareness and to recognize that even our adaptive defenses and protections can simultaneously save us, as well as keep us from being self-actualized and enlightened. It is our choice to either continue to operate from a posture of defense against the world around us, or to release the fight, flight or freeze mechanism and stand in the power of peace, joy and love.

Restore

The fourth and final phase is "**restore.**" To restore is to bring something back into its former or original state or place something back in a person's possession. One of the beliefs across religious and spiritual communities is that when someone loses their connection to Spirit, if they are to find their way back, they must first reconnect to the internal (true self) and then reestablish communication with the Source (God) in order to restore order and create balance. It is also believed that the spiritual and earthly realms must work in concert with one another in order to establish and maintain alignment. The current state of the ecosystem and the weather patterns on earth are a prime example of this truth as Mother Earth is working overtime to restore what mankind has destroyed. The planet is engaging in a massive systemic purge in order to heal itself and that energy shift is being felt and seen across the globe. The earthquakes, tsunamis, volcanic eruptions and unusual climatic phenomena that we have been experiencing over the past few decades are the Great Mother's way of restoring homeostasis. However, she will not be able to execute this monumental task of restoration by herself. Some of the restorative work must be done by mankind if balance is to be restored. If the earth has a built-in mechanism for restoration, then humanity, who is part of the circle and cycle of life, possesses the same ability. Our bodies are a reflection and a replica of the planet and, just like the Earth, when our systems are disrupted by toxicity, abuse and mismanagement, some specific measures must be employed to set things straight.

In some spiritual circles it is believed that the way to achieve restoration is to first confess (share and declare your story) and then engage in the acts of surrender, sacrifice and rededication of your body, mind and spirit to the Creator. Beloved, there are many ways to restore ourselves to the beauty and majesty that is the birthright of every human being. Whatever pathway to enlightenment you employ, when you purge or remove the debris and residue from your vessel (body temple), the space that is cleared can be re-filled and replenished with the fertilizer for your continued growth and expansion. When you are awake and in alignment with Spirit, your spiritual body detects imbalance and seeks to remove or transform it. The excavation and renovation of your vessel provides a clearing for the ingredients that will recalibrate the spirit and lead you down the path where your destiny awaits you.

The sections in the book entitled Visions of Illumination and Lightwork Affirmations have been included to support you as you transition from release to restoration. Additionally, all of the supporting spiritual elements and practices that you chose to incorporate as you continue your lightwork journey will keep you grounded and open to receiving the messages and the blessings that the Creator has in store. Beloved, as you begin to walk down this illuminated path, know that this formula is not designed to be a one-shot deal. This life-affirming regimen is to be adopted as a way of living for those who are invested in transformation, not as an ointment or a temporary remedy for the things that flare up in your world.

As you embrace this new way of being, your ego self will attempt to pull you back toward what is familiar; toward the place where the vibrations of fear, lack, greed, shame, discontent and disharmony dwell. Beloved, once again, this is part of your human experience and I encourage you to view these moments in time as opportunities to reinforce what your spirit knows to be true. As you engage in the act of living in the flesh, you will experience the tug, ebb and flow of your humanity. Your awakening is not designed to exempt you from the trials and travails of your human existence. On the contrary, your challenges here on earth create the space for spiritual enlightenment. Your enlightenment will allow you to take response-ability for your life and to live by, teach and model spiritual and universal principles. It will also allow you to decrease the time it would normally take for you to recover from life circumstances that would customarily cause mental, spiritual and emotional paralysis. As you consciously apply these rituals and teachings to your life, you will receive the support that you need to remain awake, aware, enlivened and enlightened. Beloved, I encourage you to stay the course and persevere. As you commit to walking in the light with me, the rewards will be numerous and the blessings infinite.

AFRAID OF THE DARK

Based on my mother's account and my family's confirmation, I entered the world with a dark energy surrounding me. My mother was fifteen and my father was sixteen when I was conceived. A year prior to my entry into the world, my father had impregnated another teenage girl who gave birth to a son. My conception and birth was the product of a teenage love triangle, confusion, shame, heartbreak and depression. This was the vibration that swirled around me as I grew in my mother's belly. I can recall, as a child, hearing and being told that my mother was "crazy," "loose" and "ill-equipped" to parent me. I was also told that she tried to kill me when I was in her womb and that after she went through a long, traumatic labor, she pushed out my almost ten-pound body and immediately disconnected from me. This was the foundation for the development of my relationship with my mother and it fueled my fear, judgment and disdain for her. It also created two conflicting beliefs about who I was and who I was not. I related to myself as being the "chosen one" by my grandparents and the "rejected one" by my mother.

By the time I was three years old, I had already formulated a story about life. My father died at the age of nineteen from kidney failure which was exacerbated by his heroin addiction. My mother was building a life without me and I was being sexually abused. Technically, I was a little girl but emotionally and spiritually I was beyond my years. I was carrying a heavy load that was generating fear and distrust of the world and the people in it. That fear showed up everywhere and took over everything.

At night when the members of my household were resting, I was awake. I was terrified of the dark. My tiny eyes saw big things looming and lurking in my bedroom; fear saturated my mind and my spirit. I didn't trust any space where I couldn't see who or what was coming or going. This belief was fueled by the unpredictable behaviors of adult caregivers and children in my family who did and said things that planted fear in my psyche. They focused on lack, limitations, and projected uncertainty into my mind. None of this was intentional. It was simply the formula that had existed and been passed on from generation to generation and it had an impact. These fears, low vibrational thoughts and behaviors were compounded when a family friend who was entrusted with my care and nurturance, took advantage of my innocence and the innocence of the other children in my family by being sexually, emotionally, and psychologically abusive. It was also at this age and stage that I started to wet the bed. The sexual abuse, combined with the stress and emotional wounds that I had endured, contributed to my wetting the bed several times a week and having night terrors that interfered with me getting adequate sleep. I was a restless and guarded child whose freedom was hindered by the pain that I was holding inside. My days were filled with fears of being touched, mishandled and abused and my nights consisted of dreams where I was being haunted by the man who molested me or other menacing figures who were trying to attack or kill me. I was also deathly afraid of the dark and would often lay in bed, paralyzed with terror as I waited to be dragged from my bed by a monster. For me, the bogeyman was real and every night, I waited for him to find and destroy me.

Since I had to hide from the bogeyman who came in the dark and in the light of day, I created a story to protect myself while I was asleep. I made up that if I kept my "private parts" hidden by lying on my stomach while I slept, I would be safe from harm. So on the nights that I accidentally fell asleep on my back, I would wake up with a cold, wet pool of urine on my sheets. On the nights that I remembered to sleep on my stomach, I didn't wet the bed. I was so programmed by my fear that my body was reacting even when there was no immediate danger. Despite my age, I had intuitively created a plan to simultaneously protect myself and control my body functions. I was also unconsciously training myself to activate my word through focused intention. I had an awareness that my physical body was responding to what was being done to me and I took action to counter that by using my thoughts. I realize now that these thoughts and their responses carried powerful vibrations and that they were manifesting outcomes. I learned very early that I could project my desires out into the universe and receive a tangible response.

I manifested many things by using the power of my thoughts and my spoken and written words. Some of the things that I created were dark and scary; others were edifying and uplifting, however, whatever my words produced, I knew that I was never without support. My earliest memory of spiritual support was at church. As a toddler, my grandmother took me to worship services where I was overcome by the power of the Spirit via the rituals of singing, corporate worship and prayer. I loved hearing and singing songs and the sounds of the combined voices of the worshippers. Although my family members told me that I couldn't hold a tune, I felt in my heart that I was supposed to sing to connect with God. I was aware of the power and presence of the Creator and could feel the Spirit even though I didn't know what to call it. I especially felt its presence as I played alone in the house or outdoors. I remember slipping into a trancelike state as I sat barefoot in the grass, surrounded by trees and staring up at the sky. I would be carried away by what I now know as angels to another world where I felt safe, secure and protected. They would come to me in my waking and sleeping dreams in the form of children that would nurture, befriend and protect me.

One of my "spiritual friends" was Maybee. She was an African-American girl who was a little older than me. She and I would create and play games and spend hours reading books, writing and exploring nature. Maybee also gave me the courage to speak up. She prompted me to say and do things to keep myself safe from harm. Because of her presence, I became so assertive that the man who was molesting me left me alone. I remember the last day that he violated me like it was yesterday.

My family and I were in the living room talking when he announced that he wanted to go downstairs to our basement to play pool. He grabbed my hand and announced that I was coming with him. I protested a bit and then allowed him to carry me to the basement where he placed me on a bar stool by the pool table and proceeded to play. As he hit the balls and circled the table, he would stop periodically to put his hand in my pants. I was afraid but I didn't feel as powerless as I had in the past because Maybee was there with me. She whispered to me with the voice of a woman-child that was both courageous and confident. She told me to tell him to stop and, from somewhere within me, I found the courage to say the word out loud. While I did not say it loud enough for anyone upstairs to hear, he was still visibly startled when he heard it. This, however, did not stop him from touching me again. I was terrified but with Maybee's protection, I repeated "STOP," jumped off the stool and ran toward the basement stairs. He gave chase, caught up to me when I reached the second step and grabbed my arm. He was a big man, obese, with big hands and arms. I don't know how I found the strength, but I broke free of his grip and managed to climb a few more steps when I felt his hand grab my ankle and pull me backwards down the stairs. I cried out and started to kick my feet until he finally let go. Within seconds I was back on my feet and running up the rest of the stairs as fast as I could. When I got upstairs, I didn't go into the living room to tell the adults what happened. Somehow, I knew that safety and understanding would not be provided in that space. Instead, Maybee and I went to the back of the house and hid under the bed where we stayed until he was gone. After that incident, he never touched me again but the molestation of the other children in the household continued which had a major impact on their emotional and mental states and their behavior. The things that they endured at the hands of our abuser, manifested as abuse toward me and other children. Consequently, my aunt who was only two years older than me was now acting out sexually and forcing me to engage. I held this secret for years; too ashamed, angry and confused to reveal it to anyone for fear that I would be blamed.

I carried on with my secrets safely tucked away in my heart; still seeking God's grace and desperate to be loved. One Sunday, when I was eight years old, the pastor gave the altar call and I made a decision to give my life to Christ by way of baptism. I believed that this would support me in doing what I loved to do, which was sing. I joined the children's choir and allowed the Spirit to move through me. I was determined to use my voice for God but a part of me felt out of place. Despite my acceptance into the choir, I could hear my family's voices in my head, criticizing and ridiculing me about my voice, my two left feet, and my clumsiness. I held on to these stories and was afraid that I would be discovered as a fraud. I was very insecure and confused about some of the vibes of the people that I encountered at the church. I made lots of friends but I felt some of the negative vibes that the members gave off when I interacted with them. I didn't understand these feelings; especially when the smiles that they wore on their faces contradicted what I was picking up from them energetically. Once again, my spiritual gifts revealed things that my young mind could not comprehend and I was both overwhelmed and confused.

So, during this season of my life, I attended church and spent hours on end playing outdoors and visiting with my friends on the block. I was extremely active, agile and athletic and wanted to play baseball and run track like the boys. I was academically and artistically gifted and my mind was filled with hundreds of stories of my own creation. However, none of these was enough to pull me from the dark place that I was in. At the age and stage of development when imagination, creation and fantasy are at their peak, I had already written the script, mapped out the staging, and enlisted the characters for the story that would become the foundation for my adult life. It was those formative years, between three and ten years old when my inner light began to fade and I proceeded to birth, feed and nurture the fear that would follow me for decades to come. I must commend myself for a job well done, for the entity that I gave life to festered and grew in the darkest part of my belly and eventually gained a life and a voice of its own. It quieted the voices of my imaginary friends who generated light, love and spiritual covering. The entity told me that I was ugly and it made sure that the voices of family and friends reinforced this belief. It fueled my angry outbursts and allowed my silent rage to build and gain power. It kept me from truly trusting my family and convinced me that I wasn't good enough, worthy enough or gifted enough to be of value. It told me that the only thing that I had going for me was my body and my intellect and I poured all of my energy and focus into both.

Since I had been exposed to sex before the age of five, I was preoccupied with sexual stimulation and release and I satisfied this compulsion by way of sex play with other children or through books, magazines, television or other visual aids. It was like I had a hidden radar when it came to these things as I was able to find girls and boys who would indulge me and materials to feed my burgeoning appetite. I also overcompensated at school in an attempt to compete with those who I believed were more valuable, intelligent or charming than me. The voice in my head lied to me again and again and I believed and internalized everything that it said because I believed that it was the only force that could keep me satisfied and safe from hurt and harm. Instead, it kept me numb, disconnected and out of alignment with who I truly was and the volume of my higher voice was placed on mute.

LIGHT REVELATION

We all have a spotlight shining on the stage of our lives. Some of us stand courageously in it as we tap into our strengths and utilize our gifts; others remain in the shadows, too afraid to access their greatness.

CHAPTER 1

"Flip the Switch"

As children, we were taught either directly or indirectly to fear the darkness. The darkness was where hidden and forbidden things dwelled; where the bogeyman lurked and monsters lived; where scary stories were told and the secrets of every man, woman and child were concealed. We believed that it was in the dark places that diabolical plans of death and destruction were fertilized, birthed and nurtured. We were reminded again and again that we would return to the darkness when our time on this earth was over and we envisioned our bodies decaying deep within the earth, devoid of life and light, without energy and essence.

Yes, Beloved, it is the darkness that we have consciously tried to avoid and it is the darkness that is at the root of most of our fears. But despite our aversion to lightless, lifeless things, it is in the darkness where most of us live and dwell both emotionally and energetically. Much of our time on this earth is spent thinking of dark things, creating dark thoughts and connecting to dark energies. Oh Beloved, you may be shaking your head at the idea of this; resisting the very thought of it because you have been taught to associate darkness with evil. However, the darkness that I speak of has nothing to do with evil. The darkness that I speak of is part of the full spectrum of choices that each of us has. It lives on the continuum that sits before us as we move, live and breathe in our worlds. Simply put, where there is light, there is its opposite. The power of the darkness and its pull on our lives is a choice that we can access and energize, or not. Our fear of the dark and so-called dark things is learned. We were taught to look for ugly, scary, hidden things in the dark and because we believe that they are there, we find them.

Imagine what our lives would be if we were not taught such things; if the indoctrination of fear and destruction was not passed on to us in stories or shared directly or subliminally through the implications of adult actions and the powerful images imposed on us by the media. If we were not taught these things, would we walk, play and live in the dark without reservation? Would we welcome it as a part of our everyday existence and come to expect it; not from a fearful place but from a place of pleasant familiarity and fruitful opportunity? I pose this question so that you might come to the awareness; so that we might embrace the possibility that we can choose to take our power back; that we can withdraw our minds and spirits from the places that have been feeding and fueling our fears and plug into the Source that is the pathway to our nourishment; the light.

The darkness is not the enemy. We have all passed through it and we have all experienced moments of growth and transformation as a result of the lessons and opportunities that it avails to us. There are many things that live and thrive in the dark. However, it is not intended for us to wrap ourselves so tightly in it that we lose sight of the awesomely edifying gift of the light: the light that illuminates; the light that reveals; the light that provides a vehicle for access to our higher selves. When we allow it to do its work, it reveals and unveils the answers to our deepest and most profound questions and creates a pathway that moves us closer to our destiny.

Beloved, we are all players on this stage called life. We each have our part to play and when the curtains open and the stage is revealed, there is a spotlight, a circle of power, for us to step into. Some of us rush into the light, prepared to speak our lines and play our parts. We step out boldly for we know who we are and we embrace the part that we have been ordained to play. We present the monologues, the dialogues, and the choruses in partnership with the souls that are part of our journey and we carry out each role with power and purpose. Then there are those of us who choose a different path. When the light of life appears, we miss or ignore the cue. When the curtain opens and the spotlight hits the stage, we stand in the wings frozen in place; shaken by the magnitude of the work that we are called to do in this incarnation. We cling to the darkness and remain behind the scenes for fear that the world will devour us if we step out into the light and dare to shine.

Beloved, whatever position or mindset we are operating from, it is all about choice. We can choose to cloak ourselves in the darkness as we have been taught to understand it and turn a deaf ear to the universal call, or we can step out onto the stage and walk into the light that will move us onward, upward and forward. Whatever the choice, there is no judgment in the realm of the universe, for it is designed to embrace and support us in every way. From the day of our births until our time on earth comes to an end, the spirit will remind us and nudge us in the direction of our purpose. We may resist and ignore it, but the mantle will always be ours to take up or to leave behind as we wish.

It is never too late to step out of the darkness and activate the intention for our lives. I am a living testimony that the switch can be flipped and the light activated at any time. For most of my life, I have walked on the dark side. I have unconsciously and consciously resisted my destiny even during moments when the signs were hitting me square in the face. Just like some of you, I have remained in the wings when the spirit attempted to move me forward. I've allowed intellect and logic to dictate my life and I've ignored the spiritual gifts that were boiling feverishly within me. It wasn't until my mid to late thirties that I truly woke up from a self-induced coma to discover who I truly am: a healer, chosen vessel, anointed and appointed from conception to do a greater work in the service of the world. My awakening came in waves and is still occurring every day; as will yours if you permit it.

Beloved, as your soul begins to stir and you hear the sound of the spiritual alarm in the core of your heart, resist your urge to return to the dream state that you have been dwelling in. Allow your spiritual eyes to be opened and the light to reveal the higher truths about yourself, the world and the universe. As you step into your power, you will begin to feel your affinity for the light. As you surrender to it, you will discover that you and it are, and have always been, One. As you experience the power and gain mastery over its use, you will feel the light coming out of your pores and enveloping you. As you raise your vibration and consciousness, the light will show up everywhere and you will walk and dwell in it for the rest of your days as a matter of choice. Beloved, I extend this invitation to you and I welcome you to the threshold of the powerful life that has been waiting for you. Let us walk in the light of our power, purpose and passion together and watch as the darkest parts of ourselves bow down to our illuminated spirits.

LESSONS FROM THE LIGHT:

1. An illuminated path is one that allows you to see your destiny laid out before you and powerfully choose to walk, skip, run or leap boldly toward it.
2. Light is nurturing, edifying and revealing.

3. Lightworkers willingly and sacrificially expose themselves to the world so that others may be enlightened.

VISIONS OF ILLUMINATION:

As each of the layers of this message lands and rests on your spirit, still yourself and allow the words to saturate your skin and seep into your pores. Actively engage your spirit in the action of scanning your body from your crown to your feet. Look for the areas where the dark, low, vibrations of resistance are hidden. Move slowly through each part of your vessel and locate the places that are holding your pain, holding your anxiety, holding your worries and your fears. As you identify the resistance, envision yourself placing your hands on the areas where it exists. Feel its texture and its mass; experience its heaviness and the draining nature of its presence in your body. Think about how holding this energy has impacted your mental, spiritual, physical and emotional make up. Reflect on how long it has been there and how much space it has taken up. Has it overshadowed your thoughts and desires? Has it burdened your heart and clouded your mind? Has it dimmed your internal flame and extinguished your light? When you've identified each of the areas and contemplated these questions, use your spiritual strength to begin pulling the resistance apart. Beloved, you have the power to flip the switch. I invite you to lay hands on your resistance. Gently massage each area with love and compassion. Remember that when you use the muscle of spirit, there is no anger or rage; only awareness and focused intention. Tear each layer and every piece away from your body until you have broken them down into smaller pieces. Use your hands to rip, tear and then crush the resistance until there is nothing left but microscopic particles of dust. Repeat this action over and over again until you have cleared away the dark energy from every part of your body where it dwells. When you are complete and you are left with only a pile of dust, use your spiritual voice and repeat these words again and again: "*I release all resistance into the light where it is received and transformed, and I thank you for the lessons you have taught.*" As you allow the words to permeate your soul, watch as the dark particles of resistance are lifted and then carried away into a tunnel of white light. Watch as the particles of dust are absorbed and converted into light energy and experience the metamorphosis that only spiritual transformation can generate. As the dust is carried away and your body is cleared of the debris, feel and witness the energy of your internal flame being reignited. Feel the light within you growing in heat and intensity. Feel your inner glow as it fills up the space where darkness once dwelled. Allow your vessel and your spirit to remember and reconnect with your true essence. Breathe and embrace your freedom. Breathe and experience the love.

LIGHTWORK AFFIRMATIONS:

I am covered in light and love where ever I go.

I am a powerful lightworker on a journey to freedom.

My pathway is clear; my journey is purposeful.

THE HAZARD LIGHTS

When I was in junior high school I had a group of friends with whom I spent all of my time both inside and outside of school. There were four of us and we called ourselves "Four The Hard Way." Ironically, being part of a group with this name was perfect because it reflected my angry and distant edge. I had so much that I was holding inside of me that I would constantly act out on the girls in our circle. I said and did mean things to them. Sometimes, the urge to hurt them was so strong that I felt compelled to act on it. They did not retaliate and their tolerance actually fueled my negative behavior. Because I had been on the receiving end of other peoples' meanness and inappropriate behaviors for most of my life, I unconsciously wanted to inflict pain on others. I was being ridiculed and bullied at home by my aunt and uncle who were only two and four years older than me. I felt like an ugly duckling; hopeless, useless and clueless. I was very smart in school though. In fact, I was in a class for the gifted. However, being gifted didn't make me feel more confident. It just created feelings of inadequacy about being expected to produce and having to compete to fit in.

I couldn't express to my friends why I was treating them the way that I did. I was too angry, emotionally inhibited and immature to pinpoint the reasons. I just wanted someone to pay for what happened and what was still happening to me, and they were perfect targets for my retaliation. Despite my outbursts, desire to control everything and my lack of trust, I became extremely attached to one of the girls. She and I did everything together. I started to hang out with her and her family and spent nights at her home. Things were going well at first. We went roller-skating together and attended dance classes. I started to feel happier and more at ease. My friend had a sweet disposition and she and her family were very loving toward me. However, my comfort quickly came to an end when her stepfather started touching me inappropriately and doing and saying things that were uncomfortably familiar to me. I had always been the type of child to protect myself; whether it was physically fighting back or speaking up. One day, I was forced to take action and it changed everything. I spent the night at my friend's house and when I woke up from my sleep, there he was standing over the bed with his penis exposed. He stood above me smiling with his robe hanging open. He said "Good morning" and attempted to hold a conversation with me as my friend lay sleeping in the bed, as if nothing was amiss. This was shocking and terribly frightening to me. That morning, I decided that I had had enough. He had already crossed the line so many times with his lingering stares, touches and kisses and he always found ways to invade my personal space. After his actions that morning, I could feel in the pit of my stomach that things were going to escalate. I was sad, angry and terrified. However, despite my fear, I knew that I had to do something and I did.

I decided to write my friend a letter to tell her that I would not be coming back to her house anymore and why. As I look back at the event, I know now that it was Divine intervention that led me to address the letter to my friend instead of one of the adult members of her household or mine. I taught myself at an early age that telling adults about the inappropriate behaviors of other adults yielded negative results. I believed that there was some blockage in the adult caregivers in my life that resisted the truth when it came from a child. They simply could not or did not want to hear it so I stopped confiding in them or trusting in their ability to do anything to protect me. Technically, there was no need to write the letter to my friend about her stepfather's behavior. She knew exactly what he was doing because he was doing the same things, and more, to her. But despite this, I was determined to write the letter expressing everything that I was thinking, feeling and experiencing and I gave it to her the next day. As soon as I wrote the letter, I stopped going to the house and accepting rides home from school with them. I figured I would distance myself while I waited for some sort of miracle to happen. I just wanted things to go back to normal and I waited to see if they would. In the meantime, I still saw my friend at school and we still talked as candidly as before. She was very sad about what happened and so was I. I missed the attention and the care that I received from the family but I was adamant about not going back.

A couple of days later, after we had started thinking and talking about other things, she came to school and told me that her mother found the letter in her bedroom and read it. She shared that the letter created a big uproar in her family and her mom and stepfather had declared that I was an ungrateful liar who didn't appreciate what they had done for me. I was disappointed and hurt by this but I wasn't surprised. This was the continuation of a pattern of behaviors that I grew to expect from adults.

My intuition had once again protected me from further harm: continued abuse and possibly rape. This was one of many incidents over the course of my life where my spiritual hazard lights would send out warning signals to alert me of danger and guide me to safety. Unfortunately, I also developed an unconscious belief about adults and men in particular, that would govern my thoughts and shape my decisions for years to come. I didn't expect mothers to protect or fathers to respect. I convinced myself that I could only depend on myself for protection and thus my pattern of self-reliance, isolation and emotional disharmony took root and expanded.

LIGHT REVELATION

We are all Master Teachers: We teach others how to treat us by allowing inappropriate behaviors to slide; by ignoring the obvious and pretending to be oblivious; by remaining silent when speaking up would put an end to the madness. We pretend to be worth-less and then the world joins us in that lie.

CHAPTER 2

"I Can See Clearly Now"

The human eye, that complex mechanism that activates our vision and allows us to "see" and experience the world and all of its wonders, is one of the most powerful sensory organs of the human body. The eye is remarkable as it is part of a greater system that supports the navigation and movement of our bodies within the spaces that we live and dwell. Our eyes adjust to the changes in lighting and distance and they focus on and assist us with the development of a visual record of our experiences, both great and small. When all of the components of the eye function properly, light is converted to impulses that are transmitted to the brain where an image is perceived; like a camera capturing the essence of a human face, a bird, a star in the distant sky, a tragic scene or a dangerous situation. Our eyes are also part of the system that activates our tears; the tears that cleanse, flow and release pain and joy from our bodies. Our eyes go deep and they convey a wealth of emotions that are stored within us, including the sadness or emptiness that we may feel as we experience life and living. Our eyes also reflect our heaviness, our physical and emotional dis-ease and toxicity. If you are aware and tuned in, the eyes can act as a powerful litmus test for the inner workings of our physical and spiritual bodies.

How awesome is the power of the human eye; the vessel of sight and external vision; vision that is a powerful demonstration of the Creator's magnificence; vision that contributes to the quality of life that we all experience and have grown to depend on in our day-to-day endeavors. Yes, the eyes are part of our physical navigation system. They lead and we trust. They see and we process. However, despite the miracle of our eyes and their function, they still create tremendous limitations for us that sometimes skew our perception and perspective about life, making our experiences disjointed and out of focus.

These eyes of ours, these wonderful pools of energy and knowing, can deceive and misread. It is with our eyes that we survey and assess people, situations and opportunities to determine what direction and/or decisions we should make about them. We choose mates with these eyes. We select the garments that will cover our bodies with these eyes. We assess the safety of a situation or circumstance with these eyes. We determine where we will walk, live, eat and exchange with *these eyes*.

Beloved, how often have we assessed situations, thinking that we had a full understanding of all of the nuances and all of the players involved, only to find that there were small details that were hidden from our view? How many times have our eyes deceived us and we've found ourselves in the middle of chaos, confusion and devastation? How often have we allowed opportunities to slip through our fingers because we saw them from a single, one-dimensional lens, only to discover, in retrospect, that there were multiple facets that our limited vision did not, and could not, detect?

Each of us can recall a time when we've encountered someone and decided who and what they were based on appearance, only to discover that our perception and assessment were completely off. I have experienced this on several occasions and my limited vision and focus has cost me dearly. I have made choices about who to befriend, who to follow, and who to have intimate relationships with based on my limited sight. In the midst of these choices, I found myself running into walls, drowning in my emotions, or walking on paths with poison ivy, pot holes and booby traps.

Brothers and sisters, we have relied on and journeyed with these eyes for our entire lives and we utilize them as part of a formula for elevation. However, we have also forgotten that they are just one of the many tools that we possess. As we navigate the world, we must use our physical sight, in concert with the other systems that the Creator has bestowed on us. As these systems work intimately and interdependently, they allow us to discern what direction to move in and what people and energy to connect with.

In our human frailty, we have adopted habits and ways of being that prevent us from fully tapping into the true gift of sight that we all possess: spiritual sight. This sacred vision is part of a higher system; a system that requires no gas, batteries, electrical power or circuitry. All it requires is the activation and fine-tuning of spiritual disciplines such as prayer, meditation, study and focused intention. As we exercise and engage in these acts of faith and tools of enlightenment, we heighten our awareness and expand our vision. As we tap into our "inborn" ability to see with our spiritual or "third" eye, we enhance our capacity to make choices from an elevated place.

Our spirit is the best navigation system that we can ever have. When properly fed and nourished with edifying and cleansing acts, it will reveal all and conceal nothing. When we clear the debris that has clouded our focus and lowered our vibration, we can see with clarity and precision the love and light that is availed to each of us. Our spiritual lenses will hone in on the vibrant auras and vibrations that everything and everyone possess and we will move through the world with ease. Our higher sight will identify the dim areas that cloak the people, places and things that we encounter; revealing the path, that which will steer us in the direction of our higher calling or that which will create a detour off the road to our enlightenment. Beloved, if you choose sacred sight, it will also choose you.

LESSONS FROM THE LIGHT

1. When we use our spiritual vision to "see", then our physical sight is enhanced and our insights and outcomes are expanded.
2. We all have shadowy places within us that only we can make visible. When we dare to reveal our secrets, we open up the gateway to an illuminated life.
3. When we dwell in Spirit, no person, place or thing can be hidden from our view.

VISIONS OF ILLUMINATION:

Greetings Light-Walker, I invite you to give your body permission to be at rest, to relax itself and be at ease. Use the natural rhythms of your sacred vessel to move you to a place of peace. Take air into your nostrils and release it out again as you embrace your own powerful existence in the universe. Inhale and exhale as you acknowledge your oneness with nature and allow your body to embrace its own internal flow so that it is in alignment with the rising of the sun and the chirping birds and the wind that moves through the trees. You and they are one. Breathe as you remember that you are not alone. I ask that you take in long, deep cleansing breaths as you reunite with the part of self that is fearless, that is shameless, and that is free of blemishes and discoloration. Take in a breath as you release the part of self that clings to old memories that no longer serve you. I ask that you breathe as you remember that the power of your will can transform your DNA and erase pain from your memory banks so that you can only remember joy and be energized. I ask that you breathe through your nose and take in the healing balm that the Creator has for each of us. Allow the breath to travel through your nostrils, into your airway where it will rest in your lungs. I ask that you let this sacred breath massage and clear your lungs so that you can breathe more easily and stand in your truth with power. Allow your chest to rise and fall as you breathe in the breath of life and permit the dust and the blockages to be shaken loose and released. Breathe out as you allow those impurities to escape through your nose at a pace that you can manage. Know that your healing and transformation will occur at your own rate and that you are supported regardless of your pace. You can move quickly. You can move at a medium speed. You can glide in slow motion. Whatever the pace, know that you are loved as you say "yes" to your new beginning. Steady yourself and allow the rhythms of the universe to merge with your internal mechanisms. In this moment in time, surrender to the will of the spirit and connect as a body of unity, a body of love, a body of interconnected beings having a singular experience in time. As you take in these words, allow your higher self to guide you to the sacred place within you. Beloved, I invite you to continue to breathe steadily and to release your pain, your hurt, your feelings of loss, abandonment and betrayal and embrace your power to speak, to be, and to see clearly what the universe has in store.

LIGHTWORK AFFIRMATIONS:

I expose myself to expand myself.

I seek and I see only that which will elevate me.

I choose to see love in everyone and everything.

TOTAL ECLIPSE OF THE HEART

Early one Sunday morning, my grandmother told me to go to the store to get the newspaper before we left for church. I really didn't want to go but I didn't have a choice in the matter. So I got myself together, got the money and headed out. I always felt good when I was outdoors and I remember it being a warm, breezy day. I allowed the crisp air to carry me forward as I made my way to Mr. Gilliard's corner store. When I got to Gilliard's, they had no more copies of the Daily News so I decided to walk another three blocks to another store in the neighborhood. I took my time walking down Farmer's Boulevard, the main strip that ran through my neighborhood of St. Albans, Queens. I was lost in thought as I listened to the tap of my church shoes against the pavement and the sounds of the community that I knew so well. It was just another Sunday morning and just another walk to the store until I noticed the long black limousine that pulled up to the curb on my left. The windows of the limo were tinted and I wondered who was on the other side of the glass. I decided to slow my pace so that I could get a glimpse of who was in the car when the doors opened. I was thinking that it might be someone famous. It didn't take long for me to get my wish. Within seconds, the rear door swung open and I got a full view of the two people in the back seat. The first was a tall man. He had a solid build and a grimace on his clean shaven face that spoke volumes. The second was a woman. I gasped as I looked upon her swollen, discolored and mascara-streaked face. Her eyes were puffy and red from what was probably a combination of tears, physical trauma, terror and pain. Despite the swelling and discoloration, I knew that face. It was as familiar to me as my own. I knew the hair, the shape of the head, the slope of the shoulders and the muscular frame. It was my mother; my mother who had left me with my grandparents when I was a baby to start a new life with my sister and brother's father. My mother was beautiful, yet unpredictable; youthful but unstable and volatile. By the time I was 12 years old, I had no emotional connection with her; at least, not a positive one. She would come to my grandparents' home to visit with my siblings but her presence would often generate upset and chaos in the house, especially between her and my grandmother. She would sometimes get upset and threaten to take me away from them and this angered and terrified me because I knew what type of life my younger brothers and sister were experiencing in her home and I didn't want that for myself.

I had a story about my mother that was unshakeable. By the time I was in junior high school, she had been married, divorced and had four other children. I loved my sister and brothers dearly and I loved spending time with them when they visited my grandparents' home in Queens but I hated going to my mom's house to see them because I never knew what to expect from her. She was flighty and her moods would shift on a dime. She could be emotionally explosive, volatile or depressed all in one sitting and I didn't have the experience that my siblings had with navigating that energy and these behaviors would either be toned down or exacerbated by her unstable relationships with men. I was not accustomed to dealing with that type of energy and because I was outspoken, I would sometimes say or do things to trigger her anger. Sometimes when I would visit her, she would leave us unsupervised in her apartment for a couple of days while she went to hang out with friends or boyfriends. My sister and brothers were used to this so they would scrap together meals and teach me how to manage in the house without an adult presence. I would, in turn, use my creative gifts to make up stories and games to keep them occupied and to calm my anxious mind and spirit. There were also the stories that my family told about my mother that prevented me from getting close to her.

I really didn't know my mother and, based on my experiences with her, I didn't want to know her. At a very young age, with the help of the family, I created a story about my mother and who she was. This story grew in size and dimension as I watched her navigate relationships and connect with nefarious characters that had less than honorable intentions for her and my siblings. I watched her struggle with her own sanity which manifested in unpredictable and abusive behaviors toward my siblings and others. She was a child raising children and her posture was that of someone who was wounded and ready to attack to prevent further injury. My young mind processed these scenarios as only an immature mind could and every time she spoke or I received news from family about her status, I released another part of my mind and my psyche that related to her as "mother."

So on that crisp, Sunday morning with the breeze against my back, I continued to walk, almost in slow motion, as I scanned the scene. My eyes met hers and in that brief moment, I felt a chill in my body and a part of my heart shut off. My mother, slumped in the back of this luxury vehicle, looked like the opposite of what she and this vehicle were supposed to represent. She looked shocked, hurt, embarrassed and ashamed to see me, but none of that mattered to me. My heart completely closed in an instant and a total eclipse of light and love took its place. In that moment, I became a senseless, sightless witness; disconnected from her humanity and her God-given right to be seen. This story, and others like it, became the backdrop for my relationship with her. I saw her through a lens of emotional instability, violence, dishonesty, addiction, abuse and neglect and as I grew, I struggled to do, and be, the opposite of what I believed her to be. I refused to SEE my mother and anytime something in my own behavior resembled hers, I tried to squash, reject and deny it. I refused to WITNESS my mother's humanity and, therefore, I could make her a monster and hate, berate and ignore her. I made her invisible in order to alleviate my shame and to diminish the pain that I had internalized. As a result, I became invisible as well.

LIGHT REVELATION

In any given moment, we are exercising our human capacity to witness, analyze, assess, and take action. However, much of what we think and do is on automatic pilot and is part of a script that we created during our childhood. Beloved, let's challenge ourselves to think, speak and act anew, by examining our behaviors, identifying their origins, and releasing the hold that they have on our hearts, our heads and our spirits.

CHAPTER 3

"Can I Get a Witness?"

If a tree falls in a forest and no one is present to hear it, does it make a sound? This philosophical question has been presented again and again by the most prominent and intellectually savvy scholars on the planet and fuels questions and confusion regarding observation or witnessing, and the concept of reality. It is a question that has fueled a major inquiry into the power or purpose of "seeing" and being "seen" and, therefore, the declaration that something or someone is REAL and worthy of our attention and focus. Can we assert that if no one is around to see, hear, touch or smell a thing, then it does not exist? Some would say yes. And then there are those of us who have seen and experienced a person or a thing that activated each of our senses, and we dismissed the experience and declared to ourselves and to the world that it never occurred. Sometimes, Beloved, having and being a witness makes a thing real even when we don't want it to be.

Imagine what our lives would be like if there was no one to witness for us. What if there was no one present to observe the milestones that we've achieved or to share or support the births, the graduations, the weddings, the promotions, the losses, the gains, the expressions of joy, love, sadness and rage? If there was no one there to witness them, would they be real? Do these happenings only exist when two or more are in agreement about the occurrence and its meaning? Do sound, experience, and life occur even without an audience to hear, see and respond to them?

Beloved, your reading of this book may be the result of the formula of witnessing, sharing, listening and observing that can breathe life into a "thing" and give it depth, meaning and movement. Perhaps you heard about the book from a friend and upon hearing their experience and the impact that its contents had on their lives, you decided to create an experience for yourself to parallel theirs. Your natural ability to witness and observe created a reaction that generated another reaction which, if it did not occur in time and space, you might be doing something else in this moment.

Much of what we do, say and feel is validated by the presence and agreement of others. The simple exchange of non-verbal communication such as eye contact, facial expression or touch, enhances our understanding of ourselves, the world and our purpose in it. If being and having a witness was not important, then we would have little to no use for human exchange and we could focus our energies solely on ourselves. From the time we exit the womb, we have a need to be seen, heard and acknowledged by others. If this were not so, then infants would thrive even if they didn't receive attention, nurturance and sustenance from their caregivers. Scientific research has revealed that babies that do not experience touch and energetic exchange from a living being fail to thrive.

When researchers substituted a live monkey mother with a cloth mannequin wired to dispense food, they found that the absence of the physical touch and interaction of a living being had such an adverse effect on the baby monkeys that they began wasting away and eventually died. Beloved, this study demonstrates that we are simply not wired for disconnection and isolation. Our earthly experience is designed to be a communal one where we are to see and be seen, to witness and be witnessed. These subtle yet powerful transactions are the fodder that nourishes and expands us as human and spiritual beings. I am, because you are; you are, because I am. My survival is undeniably tied to yours.

Ours is not a solitary walk. While we may experience moments where we must separate from others in order to go deep within ourselves to find answers or to commune with the Creator, this is not intended to be a practice without end. These moments of solitude and reflection are intended to grow us so that our deeper awareness of "self" can positively impact our relationships with the collective. The Creator intended for us to stand and act, not only from the position of the observer, but also from the position of the observed. If we view everyone that we encounter as our reflection, then we understand that we learn the most about ourselves when we allow others to "*see*" us, really and truly "*see*" us.

Our learning increases a hundredfold when we are open to seeing ourselves through the experiences of "others." It is through the power of witnessing that we gain the most insight. It is through our silent, motionless and focused observation that we connect and expand. Beloved, I invite you to embrace the posture of a "witness" for there is great power in witnessing. When we witness, we demonstrate our ability to connect, our capacity to stand in, and our power to make the invisible visible and to acknowledge the presence of another. It is through the intimate exchange between the observer and the observed that we can find the power of spirit and the oneness of the collective.

You may consider yourself to be a master at witnessing because you silently watch and observe others all the time. However, the witnessing that I speak of is beyond your silent, watchful gaze. Quiet observance does not always equate to full engagement or investment in the act of "seeing" and "supporting" someone as they navigate life. Many of us believe that paying attention is enough. However, just because we are physically present does not mean that we are engaging in the act of sharing ourselves or our energy. So much of our time is spent interpreting, analyzing, assessing and judging the people, places and things that we encounter in the world. We are so wired to do this, and our actions are so habitual that we're oblivious to the fact that we're responding from muscles and reflexes that we've been activating since infancy. As I shared in the introduction of this book, when we rely on our internal default mechanisms and scripts to govern our exchanges with others, we block our ability to see beyond the surface into their hearts as well as our own. This can lead to missed opportunities, misunderstandings, misgivings and missed living.

As we step into our true power, we begin to recognize the need to be fully present, open and receptive to new encounters and connections. If we want to gain full access to this power, we must be willing to take a stand for the personhood and spirithood of another. This can be achieved when we release the echoes of old stories and history that get in the way of meaningful sharing and connection. To be fully present requires that we be free of distractions and internal chatter that damage our external experiences. Our spirits, in concert and in harmony with others, create a clearing for the infinite possibilities and creations that only authentic, human exchange can render. It is the untainted, unbiased *feed-back* during these exchanges that "nourish" (feed) the soul and reflect "back" that which has been given in spirit and in truth. It is in these powerful moments of witnessing that allow each of us to fully receive the expressions and reflections that bring us closer to the Source. They also allow us to experience the fullness of who we are and why we are here. So, Beloved, as the song says, "I need you to survive." Our existence, our flesh, our humanity is solidified when we see, hear, know and acknowledge each other through an unfiltered lens. We all need a witness and we all need to witness for it is through this sharing that we can truly "LIVE" and fully "LOVE."

LESSONS FROM THE LIGHT

1. Before we can authentically respond to people, places and things, we must first be willing to remove the filters and release the stories about them.
2. Part of being a powerful player in the game of life is to value the view from the sidelines as much as the view from the field.
3. When we expose ourselves, we expand ourselves.

VISIONS OF ILLUMINATION:

Greetings Light-Walker, I invite you to close your eyes and take deep cleansing breaths as you witness and embrace the darkness that dwells there. Envision yourself as a giant balloon with no air, waiting to be filled with the breath of life. Relax every muscle as you take ribbons of air into your vessel and allow that air to fill you up. Feel your lungs, heart, chest, limbs and energy expanding as you take in air - the life-sustaining element. Feel your body filling and floating as you simultaneously sink deeper into the cushion of safety that is both holding and covering you. Allow the ground below, the air within and the air surrounding you, to simultaneously hold you up and keep you grounded. Wherever you are sitting, laying, standing in this moment, let the vibration of relaxation cover you as the air continues to fill you up. As you continue to take in air, allow the darkness behind your eyes to become more vivid. Feel the darkness swirling around in your head and experience its energy. As the darkness moves and vibrates, create a ball of white light about the size of your palm and let this energy enter the center of the pool of darkness behind your eyes. Let the ball hover, spin or bounce. You are in control of what this energy source does. You determine its brightness and the amount of heat that it produces. You are the source of this source. As the ball rotates in the darkness, witness it and breathe. With every breath, observe the ball getting brighter and the energy within it and around it increasing in intensity and vibrancy. Acknowledge the power of this ball and breathe as you accept that its power is a representation of your own. Embrace that every single cell in your body, every molecule, blood vessel, system and organ is a powerful representation of your ability to create and generate. Breathe and recognize that the element of air is working in partnership with you to support the continuation of your life force. Beloved, you are a source of power, adding energy, light and life to all of the sources in the universe. You and that ball of light moving in the darkness are manifestations of Source energy and you can choose at any time to tap in and create from that Source. With this knowledge in your mind and your heart, take another deep breath from the position of your magnificent being-ness. Experience yourself and light as one force, shifting and moving things in your world, willing your heart to beat and your blood to flow. As the ball dances in the darkness of your mind, experience its movement as part of the dance of life. Let the merging of the energy within you and outside of you, activate the systems that activate motion in your limbs. Tune into the flow of blood in your body as you float on the air that your mind is pulling into and from your lungs. Give yourself permission to witness and feel the presence of your inner being. Feel the warmth of your body and experience your inner glow; the part of yourself that resonates with the essence of spirit; the ingredients of the Creator. Breathe and take in the air as you gain awareness of your awesome SELF. You, Beloved, are a ball of dancing light; a miracle to behold and a mystery to discover and to be seen by others. Breathe and dance with the light as you witness your own power, majesty and glory. Breathe and witness the breath. Glow and witness the light. Create and witness the masterpiece that is you.

LIGHTWORK AFFIRMATIONS:

My presence is power.

I am here, I am seen, I am.

See me! I am your reflection.

THE SHADOW WITHIN

In June of 1986, two days after my high school graduation, I went away to college. I left my family in Queens to move on-campus which was only two hours away from my home. While technically I left home to begin a new part of my life, all of the old energy and echoes from my family and community traveled with me to the campus. I remember feeling on a visceral level the thick wall of pain and dark energy that accompanied me to school. When I packed my bags for college, I packed my emotional and spiritual baggage as well. I carried the pain of pregnancies and abortions, of family addiction, of the breakup of my grandparents, and what I viewed as the abandonment of my grandfather who left our family to build a life with another woman. I brought the heavy load of an abusive relationship with the boy I was with during my last two years of high school and piles and piles of secrets that were trapped inside of my womb. It never occurred to me to leave any of these behind. It had become a familiar and integral part of my being so it seemed only proper for it to move with me and take up residence in my dorm room. The ominous shadow that hovered around me was everywhere: in the air that I breathed, in the classrooms where I worked, sitting with me in the cafeteria when I ate. It kept things boiling and brewing inside of me; so much so that there were moments when I forced myself to remain silent for fear that the black sludge that was poisoning my system would begin oozing from my mouth. The level of toxicity circulating in my spirit was unbearable. However, it was all I knew. I managed to keep moving and floating from place to place like a ghost engaged in a haunting. My body was present but my spirit was detached as I went through the motions of attending classes and interacting with my fellow classmates and professors. I had grown accustomed to carrying the extra load. The dark, heavy energy that was depression, rage and low self-esteem was like an appendage, invisible to the eye but powerfully present. I convinced myself that the only semblance of power that I possessed was what I could create through my interactions with young men. They saw me, or so it seemed, and I responded to their advances by giving my body to them so that I could feel alive; like I mattered in the world. I hated myself; I saw myself as physically ugly yet they seemed to not see the grotesqueness and instead, pursued me. I realize now that they were attracted to the vibration that I gave off. Mine was the posture of the victim, the giver and the benefactor who they could extract flesh and energy from without having to replenish it. I did things to make them feel good while I sacrificed my mind, body and spirit. This was the well of confusion that I had dipped into and sipped from since high school. By the time I arrived at college, I was numb and disengaged from my true self. As campus life unfolded, I sank deeper into a malaise of self-hate and destruction. The shadowy monster who had taken residence inside of my shell of a body was in control. I became acclimated to living off the poisonous elixir that it pumped into me. Its venomous presence and the messages it whispered into my psyche kept me nourished and fed on an unhealthy, imbalanced diet of despair. By the time I was introduced to the young man who would eventually become my husband and the father of my children, I was so numb and emotionally disengaged that only fifty percent of me was present and accounted for. The other half of my personhood was saturated with rage, overwhelmed by the imbalance of unmet needs, worn down by the disappointment of broken promises, confused by feelings of loss and abandonment, and contaminated by the residue of sexual abuse and family dysfunction. During my first Christmas break from school, I attempted to go back home to Queens to be with my family and what I found when I returned was far from inviting. While it had only been a few months since I left, what I discovered was a home and community that I did not recognize and people who were worn-out, angry and volatile. What I found was a shadow of my childhood home. It was dark and the house carried the pain of my grandfather's absence, the heaviness of my grandmother's depression and the neglect of the physical space due to poverty and the infestation of my family members' crack addictions as well as the epidemic of violence and drug use in the neighborhood. The household was beyond toxic and when I came home and combined my own emotional instability with the emotional instability of my family, the blend of the energies created a huge explosion that ended with a physical altercation between me and my uncle that resulted in my grandmother asking me to leave instead of him. This ignited another level of resentment in me and after the incident; I never came home during school breaks again. I spent the next two years working on campus and/or staying with my best friend and her family.

During this time, I could barely recognize myself or my own humanity so when I met the man who would eventually become my husband, my gift of discernment was either shut off or on mute. I didn't know myself and I definitely didn't know who he was or who he was not. So I clung to him and made him, school and work the focus of my attention. I spent all of my free time at his house and even when his parents didn't know, I spent days, sometimes weeks in their home, hiding in the nooks and crannies of his room in the basement to avoid being discovered and to avoid having to go back to my family in Queens. The cycle of poor decision-making, impulsivity, deception and humiliation continued unhindered and unfettered. Our relationship was imbalanced and sometimes abusive but because I argued, fought back and "stood my ground," I convinced myself that I was okay. I broke up with him and then got back with him and then broke up with him again but the connection and the chaos remained. My beliefs, behaviors and tainted vision carried me into young adulthood and eventually, I found myself married to him, mothering, and smothering myself and others with toxicity. The marriage was the result of another unwanted pregnancy. I had broken off the relationship due to his controlling nature, instability and his substance abuse but went back after I discovered I was pregnant again. I was convinced that God would not tolerate another blatant disregard for life so I listened to the voice in my head that said "don't be like your mother," "don't have children out of wedlock," "don't be a disgrace" and it overpowered my higher voice and had me ignore the state of my relationship and my life. So despite the history and the unpredictability of the relationship I threw caution and logic to the wind and we started to plan our lives together. Part of the plan included him promising to stop using drugs and to commit to getting his life together. He chose to join the Marines and I chose to leave college and go back to the very home that I swore that I would never return. Despite my fear and apprehension, I told myself that I could go home, prepare for the baby to arrive and wait for him to send for me. While he was at boot camp in North Carolina, I got a job in a pharmacy and saved money for the baby's birth. We were married two weeks before my 20th birthday by the justice of the peace and one hour after we were married he told me and his mother that he "owned me now." Those words carried us into our lives as husband and wife and were present in the background as each of us navigated our idea of marriage.

I turned 20 in October 1988 and two months later, I gave birth to my first child; a 7lb, 13oz baby girl. Her birth was also the catalyst for my first experience with mental illness. Her entry into the world was smooth and quick. I gave birth to her without anyone present in the delivery room because she came so fast that there was no time for anyone to support or witness. The day after her birth, I remember waking up from my sleep, sweating profusely with my heart racing after I had multiple nightmares. I also remember hearing the voice of what sounded like a man in my head telling me to get my baby from the nursery and run from the hospital. I vaguely remember getting out of my bed, putting on my slippers and pushing the pole that held my IV down the hallway while I searched for the maternity ward where my baby was. I was dizzy and disoriented but I was determined to find her and flee the hospital. Thankfully a nurse spotted me and guided me back to my bed but I will never forget the intensity of the voice and the panic that I felt when I awoke from my sleep. When my husband finally arrived at the hospital, I was calmer but I still felt shaky and fiercely protective over my baby. When we were discharged and went home, I felt paranoid and suspicious of my family and friends who came to see the baby and check on me. I didn't want them holding her and I was convinced that they were there to do us harm. I never expressed this to my husband. I covered up the feelings and pretended to be okay. The voice in my head was heard one more time about two weeks after my daughter's birth. I was still staying with my grandmother and waiting for my husband to send for me and the baby so that we could start our lives in North Carolina. I was in my room watching television while the baby was asleep and my heart started beating against my chest while the voice was booming in my head. It told me to pack the baby's bag and escape from the house. This time, I knew that there was something wrong so I went to my grandmother's room, told her what was happening, laid at the foot of her bed and prayed for the voice to stop. I remained in this position for about 20 minutes while she checked in with me every few minutes to see if I was okay. As I continued to pray and ask for God's mercies, my heartbeat normalized and the voice faded. I never heard it again, but I never forgot the feeling. I had been invaded and in that moment I felt powerless and out of control. I decided to put the remnants of that night behind me and when it was time for me and the baby to reunite with my husband, I did just that. I filed it away and left New York to build a new life in Camp Lejeune, North Carolina.

LIGHT REVELATION

Unresolved trauma can lead to a slow death with no burial or ceremony. Some walk the earth having died on the inside; harboring feelings of fear, loss and powerlessness that nullify any semblance of purpose or spiritual knowing. Today, I jumpstart my heart by embracing the possibility of my transformation and claiming my DIVINE right to LIVE.

CHAPTER 4

"Toxic Tolerance"

We are all on a journey. Each of us is standing, walking or running on a road leading to a specific destination. Some of us recognize with great clarity the path that we are on and the destiny that is ours to hold and pursue; others are standing in the middle of the road of their lives, motionless and in a state of bewilderment. As we stand knee-deep in what seems like confusion, we may be unaware of how we arrived at this particular place at this particular time. We may wonder if we should double-back and retrace our steps, take a detour or sit and wait to be rescued. In these moments, it is easy to lose our sense of purpose and passion for living because the fear of failure, hurt, disappointment or disillusionment can be so devastating. These are the moments when giving up seems like the safest option and we make a choice to hand over the controls to someone or something else, instead of taking responsibility for our own output and outcomes.

We've all had moments when we've chosen to sacrifice our vision and goals because of the uncomfortable circumstances we found ourselves in. You may be experiencing one of those moments right now as you read this book. When we are experiencing challenging times we may choose to hand over the reins of our lives to someone else so that we don't have to deal or be responsible.

That choice may be fueled by feelings of overwhelm, by issues of co-dependence in our relationships with intimate partners, family members or friends or by the influence and pressure from authority figures who we believe have more answers, knowledge and skills than we do. Whatever excuses we have used in the past to relinquish our power, it doesn't serve us today to engage in the energies of self-judgment, blame or shame. The best use of our energy is to acknowledge what we have done and make a commitment to shift the pattern. It is also important to accept that part of the human dynamic involves stumbling, falling, failing and floundering so that we can discover something new about ourselves and the world. This is a gift bestowed upon us by the Creator and can be used to support us in building and sustaining a powerful life. However, the only way to discover something new about this life and this journey is to stay present, take ownership and take action.

While pain, shame and fear of the unknown are universal experiences, how we process these emotions and the experiences associated with them are as unique to us as our fingerprints. No two people respond to the same situation in the exact same way. Even if the responses or reactions appear to be identical, there are both subtle and distinct differences because we each possess the power to choose what the experiences mean to us. When we perceive something to be negative, we process the experience, internalize it, and then develop behaviors, responses and reactions to it that can become habitual, debilitating and TOXIC. As we develop attachments to our fears, anxieties and the stories that fuel them, we inadvertently develop a residue around our hearts that places a burden on our spirits. This impacts our daily walk, our work and our relationships with ourselves and others. As the residue thickens, we begin to move away from our natural responses to the world and the people in it, and we develop a line of defense to shield ourselves from real or perceived attacks, to initiate warfare, or to cower and shrink in the face of it. We may also develop a pattern of following others rather than leading so that we don't have to deal with the aftermath of failure or the pressure of success.

When we are driven by fear, it is convenient for us to blindly and obediently follow the plan that someone else has for our future; to abandon the pull toward our own destiny and silence the call for our lives. If you are someone who has devoted all of your time and energy to someone else; promoting their agenda, focusing solely on their vision and adopting their philosophy while you slowly lose sight of your own, then now is the time to redirect and reconnect. You may be wondering how you will move from this place as you stand motionless on your own life path. You may be too fearful to breathe, think or act. You may even be asking yourself how you can possibly get back on track when you have been moving in the wrong direction for so long; too stubborn to turn back and too disillusioned to chart another course. Or you may wonder how you can reclaim your own destiny as you stand in the shadows of those who you have allowed to commandeer your power.

Beloved, as you question, wonder and lament over your current reality, the answers seem beyond your grasp. The pain and confusion has left you in a state of deep despair and has resulted in you giving up on some key pieces of your life. You simply don't believe that anything can shift the circumstance in the direction of light, positivity or resolution. But I'm here to share with you that that there is a powerful concept that will reset your internal navigation system and support you in getting back to the business of living, being and doing in the world.

The answer can be found inside of you and is easy to discover if you would only allow the truth to penetrate the illusion of confusion that you have shrouded yourself in. The solution can be found in your ability to identify where your internal on-and-off switch is located; the switch that all of us have, that keeps us safe, whole, authentic and tilted in the direction of the light. So many of us have lost our awareness of its existence; it's been buried under layers of conditioning that we have been subjected to since childhood. We've been trained to take in and synthesize pain and to allow it to live inside our bones, our arteries, our organs and our sacred energy centers. We listened to, and internalized, the messages that our caretakers, our teachers and our peers poured into us and we started to believe that pain, confusion, negativity and denial were the norm; like vitamins to ingest as part of our daily regimen.

As a result of this indoctrination, we have become human shock absorbers. Our bodies are conditioned to soak in and activate sickness, doubt, fear despair and dis-ease. We are conditioned to expect things to go wrong and our tolerance for toxic energy has us wired to attract negativity like a magnet. We feed on the toxins and our tolerance grows and grows until its vibration extends itself outside of our bodies, spinning and vibrating on its own axis. This toxic tolerance keeps us tied to relationships where we are being abused; living in homes that are cluttered and where the stagnant energy disrupts our sleep and throws off our equilibrium. It keeps us on jobs where we are overworked, underpaid and mistreated and it keeps us in a never-ending cycle of lack, loss and limbo.

Beloved, you do not have to remain in a toxic state. There are spiritual, emotional and physical regimens for detoxification that can move you from a place of internal discord to a place of balance and peace. Because of your awareness of the imbalance that exists in your inner and outer auric space, your journey of transformation has already begun. Your awareness is the catalyst for your metamorphosis. There are many who live in a deep well of denial, where the ingredients for spiritual awakening cannot be seen, felt or heard. Now is your time to release resistance and to embrace restoration. As you create a formula for transformative living, you will clear the way for your mind, body and spirit to flush out the noxious energy that has been residing in your psyche and contaminating your vessel.

Beloved you have spent a good portion of your time and energy building your tolerance for toxic mind, body and spirit exchanges and the same energy that you used to build it, can be used to dismantle it. A slight shift in focus can create the fertilizer to move you in the direction of elevated living. My transformation was initiated by a single choice that totally shifted my energy. One day, after days and days of experiencing anger, depression, sadness and despair, I heard the voice of my eldest child in a way that I hadn't in the past. I took an action that day that was different than all of the days that preceded it and my life hasn't been the same since. When I finally made the choice to do something different, a new ingredient was added to the mix of my life that shifted everything. This ingredient set the stage for a new recipe for living to unfold. Without my full knowledge or understanding, it moved me in the direction of my transformation and helped me to recognize my true self.

You, too, can find and activate the button that will recharge your spiritual battery. Perhaps you can read a book, attend a workshop, take a class or identify a regimen that moves you (prayer, meditation, yoga, exercise, therapy, Reiki, journaling, church, singing, and drawing). Maybe you will choose to get up one morning before daybreak to watch the sunrise and, as a result, you will recognize the beauty of life, including your own. Whatever the ingredient is, make a choice and then take a step. The Universe has a beautiful way of supporting us when we allow it to. So, Beloved, as you open yourself up to the possibility of transformation, allow yourself to be guided toward the people, places and things that will reveal the answers that you seek and release the toxicity from your life.

LESSONS FROM THE LIGHT:

1. Beloved, you are powerful. You had the power to create your current condition and you also possess the power to release it from your body. Release the fear; stand in your power and heal.
2. We all have a self-clearing and healing mechanism built into our spirits. This mechanism must be activated every day. We must engage in clearing our sacred vessels from the tolerances that have built up in our bodies as we move around in our worlds.
3. No one can depress you. No one can make you anxious. No one can hurt your feelings. No one can make you anything but what you allow inside. It is what we tolerate that makes us toxic.

VISIONS OF ILLUMINATION:

Greetings Light-Walker; BREATHE. Take air into your vessel through your nostrils and release through your nostrils. Feel the mechanism of your respiratory system as it does the work that it is designed to do. Imagine the element of air, the representation of thought, speech and creativity circulating in your lungs. Experience the rise and fall of your chest cavity and abdomen as you relax into your magnificent body. Whatever the physical challenges—whether its fatigue, muscle tension, a cold, asthma or hypertension—see and relate to your body as the perfect and exquisite vessel that the Creator designed it to be. View your form as an extension of the Earth, perfectly shaped and molded by the power and magic of the elements and connected to the ebb, cycle and flow of the Universe. See your existence as an integral part of the circle of life and rejoice in your placement and your purpose. As the breath circulates in your body, imagine the internal flow of the molecules of water that are moving within you. The element of water fuels your emotions and provides the fertilizer for growth and expansion. See yourself as part of the vast ocean of life that we are all contributing to and allow yourself to float in the power and might of it. As you activate the healing waters of your vessel, embrace the warmth that exists within you. Feel your internal flame and the heat of the blood and the chemical reactions that generate fire in your organs and limbs. The element of fire, the purifier and creator of passion and pleasure, is alive and churning within you. Envision yourself as the lava at the core of the planet, producing energy and providing internal and external movement and stability. As you wave your fiery wand across the terrain of your vessel, relax in the power of your creative flow. As you breathe and create balance in your body, envision the element of Earth nurturing, grounding, fertilizing and sustaining life. Experience your flesh and the contours of your body as the container for all things. See yourself as mother, father, friend and companion to everything that is above, below and beside you. And as each of the elements merge together in perfect form, remember that you possess all of the ingredients to ignite your own transformation. You are the alpha and the omega of your own journey towards enlightenment. So as you breathe and manifest, circulate the healing waters, ignite the internal flame and fertilize the abundance within, surrender to the process of your own awakening and discover that you are the answer.

LIGHT WORK AFFIRMATIONS:

I choose.

I let go.

I am healed.

A WALK ON THE DARK SIDE

By my early to mid-twenties, I was operating on automatic pilot; convinced that I was doing what I needed to do to build a life for myself. It was my belief that every casualty on my path, whether friends, family or intimate partners, were victims of their own weaknesses and if I did anything to hurt them, they somehow had it coming. If anyone experienced my wrath, I felt that it was a justified response to a personal or energetic attack on me and, of course, I had to defend myself. The mantra that I adopted during this period of my life was "never regret anything that you do" and I vowed to maintain this so that I didn't have to feel, do or change anything.

Life as a married, military wife was filled with disappointments, sacrifices and loads of chaos. I was elated to be a mother but disenchanted with my environment and my role as a wife. I felt trapped, unappreciated and disrespected by my husband. I did what I knew to do to shift things: resist, debate and attack. I had always been a free spirit, making my own decisions, my own money and creating my own path. Life in North Carolina was boring, mundane and slow. My resentment grew daily as I tried to convince my husband to teach me how to drive our car or to take me places where I could be around other people. Before we moved into military housing, we lived in two locations; one of which was a trailer park on the outskirts of town that was only accessible by car. We lived there while waiting to be approved for military housing. Day by day, I felt myself wasting away. I felt isolated and had to depend on my husband for everything including my clothing, travel, personal products, money and recreation. The amount of control that he had over the finances, transportation and our living arrangements was creating a rift in an already shaky relationship. As each day rolled by, I found myself longing to return to New York or to be in school where I felt productive and alive. When I spoke to him about these things, he seemed defensive and uninterested which increased my resentment and deepened my desire to get away. I tried to distract myself by cleaning, playing with the baby, reading book after book and watching television. All of these activities did nothing to mitigate my boredom and my intense feelings of regret. My frustrations and upset were triggers for my husband and would lead to arguments and/or physical altercations. By the time we moved from the trailer to the military housing, I was so numb from the emotional highs and lows that I was retreating into myself; isolating and insulating myself against an environment and a relationship that I didn't want to be in.

Shortly after we moved, I found out that I was pregnant and I was devastated. I did not want to have another baby. I begged my husband to let me terminate the pregnancy but he refused, saying that he never wanted to do that again and that I/we were going to have the baby no matter what. So I went on with the pregnancy but I was very depressed and angry. I felt trapped and disconnected from all emotion while I waited for the pregnancy to be over. My husband's behavior at this time was confusing. Nothing that he did or said was congruent with a man who wanted another child. In fact, he told his mother that he didn't understand why I kept multiplying and had done nothing to prevent my pregnancies. This upset me because it implied that I was solely responsible and it caused me to think about how irresponsible I had been with my body and my vision for myself. My misery showed up everywhere and I barely did the things that I knew to do except take care of my daughter. I started pre-natal care late and lied to the doctor about how I was managing my health. I barely called anyone in my family and I did nothing to prepare for the impending birth.

I went into labor shortly after my husband and I took a trip to Georgia to visit his brother and my best friend. They were also a military couple and the drive to the city that they lived in was long and hard on my body. I was seven months pregnant then and I remember feeling excruciating pain and tightness in my belly. We drove for several hours and I could not find any comfort no matter what position I took but I remained silent through it all. When we finally arrived, I could barely walk. As soon as my best friend saw me, I could see and feel her worry. She questioned my husband about my appearance and kept checking on me every few minutes to see if I was okay. I was in a lot of pain but I minimized how I was feeling to keep up appearances. At the end of the trip when we were preparing to go back home, my best friend looked distraught. She rubbed my back and held my hand and insisted that I rest as much as possible. She also confronted my husband and insisted that he take care of me. The day after we returned home, I started bleeding in the middle of the night. My husband had started working a second job, driving a taxi, to earn extra money for our family so I waited until he came home to tell him what was happening. When we arrived at the emergency room, my labor was in full swing and there was nothing that could be done to stop it.

I remember the blood and what seemed like gallons of fluid coming out of my body. My husband was distraught and didn't know what to do or say. I, on the other hand, was emotionless. The birth was traumatic; not because of the labor but because of the procedures that they went through to manage the delivery of the baby. We found out that our baby had a birth defect called a duodenal atresia and had to be flown by helicopter to a hospital in another city for surgery to connect her stomach to her intestine. We saw the baby for about 30 minutes before she was rushed away. There was no time for parental bonding; no time for recovery; no one to check on me or my husband or to ask us questions about our mental or emotional states. Something broke within me when I gave birth to my daughter. The woman who left the hospital was a shell of a person, moving in suspended animation as everything around her was spinning out of control. When we finally saw our baby again, it was a day later and she was about to have surgery. We went to the neo-natal unit to visit her and I did not recognize her when we arrived. She looked different from how I had remembered her. She lay in bed with tubes in her body and an oxygen mask on her face; I was convinced that this was not my baby. The thoughts that flowed through my head seemed real to me and all I kept thinking was "Where is my real baby? Who has my little girl?" I didn't know that I was mentally off-balance. I didn't want to tell my husband how I was feeling or what I was thinking. I felt alone and in that moment, I chose to endure on my own.

We stayed at the Ronald McDonald House for three weeks until she healed. While we were there, we went through the motions of caring for our baby. As each day passed, I remained silent as my thoughts continued to run in the direction of a mental break. When she was finally discharged, it was Christmas Eve and we were finally a family of four that looked normal on the outside but was erupting on the inside. My husband returned to regular duty and I was left to care for these two babies on my own. The experience with the new baby was totally different than my experience with my first child. She did not get up for feedings. When she did, she drank very little milk. Because she was premature, she was delayed in her development. I barely picked her up and felt frightened and shaky when I held her. I spent most of the first several months afraid that I was going to do something to hurt the baby or myself. Since these issues were never acknowledged or discussed in my family, I had no clue that the women on my mother's side experienced depression and sometimes psychosis after giving birth. I discovered that the condition went as far back as my great-grandmother who I knew was mentally ill but never inquired about her history or the onset of her condition. I didn't ask questions because the women in my family knew how to protect their secrets.

Before my second daughter was born, I didn't believe that it was possible for me to have a baby and not nurture it or provide motherly love and affection. So when she arrived and I had no maternal connection to her, I felt tainted and flawed as a mother. I kept these thoughts, and the reality of my situation, hidden away where all the "bad things" about me were buried. Our saving grace was that her sister was a toddler and moved around a lot so I spent a good portion of time supervising her activities. I also had a neighbor and another military family who came over to visit us on a regular basis. This kept me from becoming totally unhinged.

I was able to remove myself from this potentially volatile situation when I got called to do work for the United States Census Bureau. The work was short term but I was thrilled to be out of the house and away from what seemed like a disaster waiting to happen. My neighbor agreed to keep the children while I worked and I quickly threw myself into the experience. I was finally doing something where I could use my brain and I was making my own money. This caused a problem with my husband because he wanted me to give him my checks and I refused. Our relationship was growing more toxic by the day and it came to a head one afternoon when he came home early for lunch. We got into an argument that escalated to physical violence. I called the military police and the matter was immediately turned over to his commanding officer who reprimanded him. However, I knew that this was not the solution for him or for me. I knew that I had enough and I wanted out but I had no idea how I would make it happen with two children and limited resources.

The answer came by way of the Gulf War when my husband was deployed to the Middle East for several months. While he was gone, I was free to go where I wanted to go and do what I wanted to do; I went haywire. I didn't care what anyone said; I was committed to living my life by any means necessary. Any means necessary meant leaving the children with a neighbor while I went to the club. I would go out with other military wives and we would govern ourselves like we were single women and hooked up with men. In the midst of my club hopping, I met several brothers who didn't care that I was married because I didn't care that I was married. I had a persona for both my day and night life and I played each part to the hilt. I even traveled back and forth from North Carolina to New York so that I could elevate my excitement and reconnect with the life and the people that I missed so much. Nobody could tell me anything and none of the people around me could stop me or check me because they were of the same mindset. Then I met someone that I believed would rescue me from the life that I no longer wanted to live. I started treating him like he was my mate and contemplating my great escape from my husband. I was irresponsible and disrespectful as I moved around our small town flaunting this relationship for the world to see. Meanwhile, I was receiving and writing letters to my husband and pretending that all was well at home. When I finally got the news that he was coming back home, I panicked. I didn't know how to return to the life as his wife and I didn't want to. It was all about me. My thirst for freedom could not be assuaged.

During this season of my life, I had two small children and no idea what was coming next. I had made another series of impulsive decisions and was fantasizing about the outcome instead of looking at the reality of my situation. I had no insight into my emotional or spiritual instability or state of mind as I transitioned from life as a military wife to life as a civilian mother and lover. I had no clue that I was in the throes of a chemical imbalance and I was making choices inside of the haze of my condition. Once again, I was wearing a mask and pursuing a better life while a tsunami of emotions was brewing in the background and foreground. I was having another overlapping love affair where I convinced myself that my suitor would swoop in and save the day. I swore that this person was my soul mate and that we would stay together forever. When I left the toxic marital situation that I co-created in North Carolina, I felt that I was doing the right thing because I was being abused. When my husband was deployed to the Middle East, I used the freedom as an opportunity to plan my exit strategy. I resolved in my mind that I would finally get a chance to experience "true love" in my life and I declared to God that I deserved some happiness with someone who loved and respected me.

So on the 6th day after my husband returned from his deployment, I found myself back in the same pattern of denial, defensiveness, deflection and disconnection. But I had a plan and I was determined to carry it through. Before the end of the day, without clear thought or hesitation, I had packed my children's and my belongings and left our home to stay with a friend. My husband was shocked and devastated to say the least, but my wiring for escape had already been tripped and there was no putting it in reverse. I left my marriage feeling justified and relieved. I didn't think about the impact, nor did I take responsibility for breaking another heart, bruising another spirit or dishonoring another sacred contract. After a short visit to New

York, I moved to Savannah, Georgia to get a fresh start at the behest of my best friend. Her husband, my husband's brother, was also deployed and so she offered to let me stay with her until I got on my feet and could get my own apartment with the children. She also gave me a job as a part time substance abuse educator and prevention specialist.

Eventually, I was joined in Savannah by my new mate, the man that I had cheated with and who I was convinced had "saved" me from the life that I was living. This man supported and nurtured me as I got back on my feet and I was convinced that he was my savior and that we would be together forever. I had no idea that the cycle that I created as a child to manage my life had a gravitational pull that I didn't know how to shift. My new life was only a replica of the old life; it was just more polished with a new set of players in a new setting.

I swore that things were different and that my life was on an upswing. My new mate was the opposite of what I had experienced in other relationships. He was generous, loving, supportive, open and committed. Life was good for a while but regrettably, it didn't take long before the feelings of low self-esteem, anger and victimhood started to take over again, and my old patterns resurfaced. During that season of my life, I had a vague awareness of those patterns but it was too painful for me to let myself see it in is fullness. There was so much guilt and shame but I couldn't allow it to come to the surface so I ignored the signs and I dismissed my intuition when it attempted to reveal things to me.

My intuitive gifts were always present as a vehicle for awareness and release, but my denial and depression kept me from hearing and receiving the messages they would bring forth. Even when the new relationship began to unravel due to the lies, improprieties and imbalanced living, I was in denial about the part that I played in it. I didn't want to see who I was. I couldn't admit that I had developed a pattern of engaging and disengaging in intimate partnerships and emotionally distancing myself from the men and women, who wanted to love, befriend and support me. I didn't trust others because I didn't trust myself. I thought that I could fake my way through everything and, therefore, the life I created was one-dimensional at best. So when yet another relationship ended I shut another emotional door and convinced myself that everything that I did to contribute to its demise was provoked or justified. Sound familiar?

I vividly recall an incident during this phase of my life when the Creator attempted to throw me a life line and save me from myself. One morning, I was driving to work when, out of nowhere, a wave of intense energy flooded my entire body and filled up the air space in the vehicle. I was so overwhelmed by its presence that I had to pull over on the side of the road for about 30 minutes to attempt to regroup. As I sat in the car, I prayed and cried and promised God that I would acknowledge the spirit and turn my life around. I knew with every ounce of my being that I had had a visitation and that the Creator was speaking to me, beckoning me and offering me refuge from the deep hole that I had fallen into. The intensity of the experience resulted in me finding and joining my friend's church in Savannah. I started reading the Bible, attending church on Sundays and singing in the choir; however, it simply wasn't enough. I felt isolated and alone and my negative views of myself and the world were too strong to maintain spiritual constancy. I continued to live my life as a woman committed to working and producing in the world of work. I excelled on my job, was given additional responsibility and the freedom to be creative and fully expressed. I spent my working hours counseling and supporting my clients as they navigated the challenges of life, while I remained emotionally and spiritually disjointed in my relationships with friends, family and myself. There were people in my life at that time who wanted to see me succeed and believed in me. One such friend opened her heart and her family to me and provided nurturance as I struggled to find myself again. She could see right through me and she picked up on the disconnect that I had with my youngest daughter. She saw the pain and the dark energy but she never judged, criticized or confronted me. She and her husband simply loved me for what I was and for what I was not and I loved them back the only way I knew how at that time.

I held on to my life in Savannah as long as I could and then I decided to move back to my family home in Queens, New York. I even rekindled my relationship with my last mate who had moved back to New York after our relationship ended in Savannah. As soon as I moved back in the house and started interacting with family members on a daily basis, the flashbacks from my childhood flared up. All of the old ghosts were haunting me and sleeping in my old bedroom was draining my energy and essence. I was depressed, angry, having nightmares and feeling overwhelmed by the family dynamics. Once again, my work and relationship patterns returned and I found myself seeking solace in working long hours at my new job. While I was working, I met someone new and fell into the attractive and distracting allure of new relationship. This created yet another complicated, overlapping relationship where one man was being deceived by me and the other was being pursued by me. The red flags and alarms were going off in all directions but I ignored them all and kept going full speed ahead. I continued down the road that I knew was filled with potholes and booby traps only to experience another messy ending and a toxic new beginning with someone whose emotional issues reflected outwardly what I was covering up inwardly. Soon my reconciliation with my former mate was abandoned and I started maneuvering in the dark, sneaking, lying and cheating until my entire wall of lies crumbled at my feet. Even after I was exposed as a cheat and a fraud, my mate was still willing to forgive, start over and pursue a future with me and my children but I was too entrenched in the toxic, chaotic dance that I was accustomed to so I chose to let the relationship go. I opted to do what I always did, jump headfirst into another relationship without regrouping, assessing, surveying or listening to my higher voice. I crossed over into the world of fantasy and denial and entered a union with someone who was on the rebound and was masking issues of depression and emotional imbalance. It wasn't long before these issues bubbled up to the surface and hit me in the gut but I ignored the voices of my family members and opted to go into "Ms. Fix It" mode by using my skills as counselor, case worker and professional savior as well as my mastery over the art of denial, to support my decision to stay in the relationship.

I ignored the subtle and not-so-subtle cues that surfaced in the relationship and I found justification for remaining in the union even when all of the indicators pointed to a quick exit. Instead I took the elevator up and committed myself to creating a relationship that would last; AGAIN.

My saving and stabilizing grace in the midst of my madness came in the form of an invitation from my old college roommate. She asked me to attend a service with her in Brooklyn, at her place of worship, called St. Paul Community Baptist Church. I was mentally, spiritually and energetically off-kilter at that time and desperately wanted a change of scenery and pace, so I accepted the invitation. God and church had always been my refuge, and it was my prayer that this church would help me clear out the cobwebs from my past so that I could release the negative energy that was brewing and growing inside of me. I also believed that finding a church would help me maintain my relationship and have the family life that I desperately wanted to create.

I attended St. Paul for the first time on Mother's Day of 1994 and immediately fell in love with the church. I would have joined that morning but my mate was apprehensive about it so I held back. Two Sundays after our first visit, we joined the church with my two daughters and I decided to be re-baptized as a symbol of my commitment to God. Ironically after that first Sunday in 1994, the friend who introduced me to the church never returned. It was clear that spirit provided a messenger to get me through the door of the church. Joining St. Paul was like a dream come true and I immersed myself in the ministry. I started learning about God, Black history and my culture, race, community, male and female relationships and the power and purpose of ritual. The Bible was used as a living instrument for transformation. Music, drama, the spoken word, dance and the visual arts were infused in everything that we did as part of the worship experience. I discovered who I was as a woman of color at St. Paul and my spiritual and artistic gifts were celebrated and expanded as I emerged as a leader within the congregation. The ugly, awkward, damaged little girl with two left feet and the horrible singing voice was now worshipping, co-creating, performing, singing and traveling around the country as part of a powerful healing movement. I was recognized, honored and respected in the ministry and so was my family. I spent every moment that I could in this cocoon of positive energy and love and I was healing deep seated issues as I engaged in this spiritual work. However, the love affair with the church didn't last and my interest, energy and growth started to fade. By my 9th year in the ministry something had shifted. I couldn't put words to it. I just felt that I had reached a spiritual plateau and that something was missing. While the spiritual shift was occurring, my relationship with my mate was simultaneously losing its luster. We were five years into the union and on the surface things appeared to be great. He was active in the church, committed to the relationship and devoted to the family that we had co-created, but there were problems between us that were deeply rooted in our past histories and our emotional imbalances. I agreed to go to counseling to address the issues and to salvage the relationship but, by that time, I had already left emotionally, mentally and spiritually. I stopped having sex with him, started entertaining the advances of other men, spent more time at work and at church and was in school pursuing my masters in clinical social work. The lack of intimacy, connection and physical presence was dismantling our partnership every day and thread by thread it was unraveling.

During the counseling sessions, I put on my best face. I avoided talk of marriage and the future and I convinced myself that I should stay out of a sense of obligation to him, my daughters and our church family. This was the story that I made up so that I didn't have to face reality or deal with my lies. The relationship continued for two additional years and my energy and focus turned toward other people, places and things. The old script was open, reactivated and I was playing the lead role in my own tragedy. Once again I was hiding, deceiving and making excuses while the wreckage and dead bodies piled up.

The integrity of the relationship was non-existent and my thoughts, actions and energy demonstrated that daily but I was too cowardly to come clean and too selfish to end it. However, one summer evening the end came by way of an impromptu phone conversation that he and I had while he was on his way home from work. A mundane discussion about our plans for the evening turned into a deep conversation about our relationship. He asked me about my true feelings for him and before I could think about it, I gave him an unedited answer. He asked me if I loved him and I told him that I didn't. My answer caught him completely off guard and it cut him deeply. I was shocked that the words came up and out of me but was also relieved that I had finally told the truth. I was not, however, expecting the actions that followed. That night, he came home, packed his belongings and left our apartment and I did nothing to stop him. The relationship was over in an instant and I did nothing to stop it. There was a brief moment when I considered trying to smooth it over but the thought passed as quickly as it came. Once again, my concentration was on me and I pacified myself by telling myself that I could no longer remain in a situation where I was not happy. So, he moved out during the summer while my children were visiting their father and I simply filled in the empty spaces where his presence had been, broke the news to the girls when they returned home and moved forward with my life just as I had done in the past. I told myself that I did what I had to do and I slammed the door on yet another relationship and didn't look back. In doing so, the light of my spirit dimmed and I proceeded to maneuver in the dark.

After the breakup, I returned to what I knew. I was completely wrapped up in the job and the ministry at St. Paul and somewhere, in the midst of it all, I landed right back in the center of another self-generated drama. I traveled around the country with the church, participated with the various ministries, attended services and meetings and fulfilled my obligations as a member of the congregation, but underneath the activity dwelled an unhappy, enraged soul. By year 10 of my membership at the church; I had changed but I hadn't transformed. I had grown but I hadn't let go of the story of being a damaged, ugly, worthless little girl and the power that it had over my life. My spiritual temple was freshly painted and, on the surface, all of the rooms looked polished and pristine; however, a closer look revealed that the wiring and the irrigation system was short-circuiting and malfunctioning. The system was corroded and no matter how much I polished the pipes, the outcome was still the same: backed-up sewage and debris.

LIGHT REVELATION

I am in a relationship and it's COMPLICATED. There's denial and deception, miscommunication and condescension. There are unmet needs and broken promises. There's inattentiveness and denial of affection. I'm in a relationship and it's COMPLICATED and my significant other is "ME." Before we enter an intimate partnership with "OTHER," let us first seek clarity and counsel about our relationship with "SELF."

CHAPTER 5

"It's Temple Time"

As we experience our individual journeys as spiritual beings, it is important for us to stop and survey each aspect of our lives to determine if there is balance and reciprocity in the ebb and flow of our internal power. We cannot compartmentalize spirit. It is intended to permeate every part of us and to be present in each of our interactions and relationships. When we dare to conduct a thorough and authentic inventory of our personal and spiritual walk, we may discover that our spiritual foundations have tiny cracks in them; cracks that cannot be seen with the naked eye but are present nevertheless and creating imbalance and disharmony. When we are open and committed to engaging in this close examination of our lives, we begin to notice that there are areas where our inner light and innate power is leaking out into the ether as we compromise our values, muffle our voices and deny our higher calling. This drainage depletes our energy and diminishes our life force so that the slightest application of pressure causes those cracks to become holes that, left unaddressed, will eventually lead to a spiritual collapse.

Once the tiny fissures begin to appear, small volcanic eruptions occur within our sacred energy centers. The eruptions may be ever so slight, but their impact triggers turbulence and a ripple effect that spills out over everything and contaminates our internal and external worlds. We may not notice the eruptions or the increased heat that is brewing inside. In fact, the increase in temperature may become familiar; even tolerable for us. However, over the course of time, the effects accumulate and we find ourselves neck-deep in a chasm of chaos and confusion with, seemingly, no life support to sustain us and no way to find our way back to solid, stable ground. This pool of toxicity comes in many forms and each of us knows what it looks like, sounds like, tastes like and smells like when we experience it. There are no two people who experience this in quite the same way, however, the end result is the same: spiritual disconnect and damage to the integrity of our sacred temples.

Our temples and the spirits that dwell within them are the shrines, the holy places, the sanctuaries that have been gifted to us by the Creator to support our journey on the physical plane. They are the conduits by which we connect with the spirit realm. Since our temples provide the passageway for direct communication with the Creator, the time that we spend nurturing, building and purifying them is essential to our growth, healing and enlightenment. When we neglect them and fail to create space in our lives to engage in the rituals and practices that keep the doors, walls and floors of our temples clear and clean, what accumulates within us is an energetic malaise that blocks our flow, dims our light and lowers our spiritual vibrations. A compromised relationship with spirit decreases awareness and allows mundane, distracting and disempowering thoughts and behaviors to dominate us. These lower vibrations overpower the peace, disrupt the harmony and override our spiritual programming; leaving us depleted and off-balance.

We all have experienced and overcome imbalance at some point in our lives which means that we have the capacity to recognize and address it when it rears its head. It may appear in the form of impulsive, erratic behaviors, self-sabotage, low self-esteem, arrogance, manipulation, greed, lust, self-absorption, cynicism, intolerance of others or isolation. We are also exposed to, and affected by, the imbalance of others when we are involved in relationships with toxic people and witness what they do or say that depletes and/or burdens us. Imbalance is also caused or exacerbated by what we take into our vessels in the form of food, drugs and alcohol. When we overeat, starve or abuse our bodies by filling them with things that break them down rather than build them up, then our ability to discern and process energy and information is hindered or shut off which makes us susceptible to physical, emotional and intra-psychic injury. Some of our habits, such as, overwork and over-commitment block our innate ability to read the cues in our external world. The toxicity within our temples can inhibit our ability to discern the energy and motives of others and muffles our ability to listen and hear beyond what people are saying and intuit the true meaning and motives behind their communication. This creates a form of spiritual deafness that contributes to the development of relationships with individuals, groups and communities that distract us from our purpose and takes us off course.

Beloved, whatever our default mechanisms and programming are, when our temples are dismantling, we must take action. The quality of our existence is dependent on our ability to review, reflect, release and restore the natural order of things. Restoration can take place by engaging in reparative rituals that will rebuild the pathways to spirit. I invite you to engage in a spiritual fitness regimen, just as you would if you were seeking to transform your physical body. This regimen consists of four actions that, if authentically and consistently employed, can clear the sacred space and elevate you to a place of deeper understanding and spiritual awareness. Our regimen begins with **air**; yes, air. The power of our own breath, which is the essence of life, can restore us if we would only engage in meditation and breathe work as part of our regular practice.

The power of deep, diaphragmatic breathing can do wonders for the temple and will move stagnant energy and reconnect circuits that have been broken by the mind, body, spirit disconnect that is plaguing the planet. The next part of the regimen includes **movement**. Our bodies are in constant motion and are stimulated and expanded by action. When we walk, run, dance or read edifying material, it releases blocked energy and activates the spirit. A body in motion stays in motion. Be deliberate about the moves that you make and free yourself of the cyclical lethargy that you are plugged in to. The third element of the formula for temple restoration is **nourishment**. What we ingest into our bodies can either drain or replenish the cells. Releasing toxins from our temples gives us more physical power which provides support for the activation of air and movement. And finally, we must **anoint** our temples. Anointing comes in many forms. We must set our bodies apart from that which is in the world and honor them by engaging in prayer, releasing behaviors that harm, and re-dedicating our bodies to the Creator. Beloved, the journey begins with you, with your intentions and the activation of your commitment.

LESSONS FROM THE LIGHT:

1. The body is a conductor of energy and our awareness of its power allows us to remain tuned in to what we allow ourselves to take in and release from day to day.
2. Like attracts like. Our temples draw unto us that which they reflect. When we closely examine the people and things that are currently surrounding us, we will unveil the type of temple-cleansing we need to engage in.

3. Our chakras are sacred gateways that balance out our energy and give access to the spiritual realm. Clearing these powerful energy centers allows us to generate more power and raise our individual and collective consciousness.

VISIONS OF ILLUMINATION:

Greetings Light-Walker. As you absorb the message that you just read, get settled and lean into the silence. Resist your habitual tendency to judge and evaluate content or to question whether you are getting or being something and simply allow the energy and wisdom of your higher self to reveal the places within you that require clearing and cleansing. Remember to breathe; for the breath is a passageway to a deeper level of growth and *inner*standing. As you kneel or lie on your back, allow the spirit to cover and indwell you as you absorb the message into your sacred energy center. Allow your body to sink into a state of relaxation by releasing the tension and tight spaces in your muscles, joints and heart. Relax your head and neck by letting the tightness that you have grown accustomed to holding there float away from your body and into the ether. Now that the space has been emptied out, breathe and clear away the residue from the anxiety, stress and pain that you were holding on to. Breathe and nurture your limbs, your organs, your respiratory, circulatory and reproductive systems. Allow the toxins to be purged that have been traveling along these passageways. Imagine the release of this unwanted energy. See it floating away from your body and being taken up by the Creator and transformed into light energy. Breathe through your nostrils, Beloved, and invite the air that you create and release to massage your torso, your abdomen, your waist and your hips. Use the breath of life to flush out your pores and caress your skin. Wash away every remnant of the rigid, stagnant energy that has created a strain on your thighs, knees, calves, ankles and feet. Let the extra burden that you've been carrying seep out of the soles of your feet and bid the tension farewell. Envision the last bit of tension leaving your temple and give your newly transformed vessel an energetic embrace. As you wrap your spiritual arms around yourself, experience your mind, body and spirit as the whole, complete and perfect vision that the Creator crafted them to be: free of stress, free of dis-ease, free of fatigue and imbalance. Your temple is the beginning, the middle and the end, and you are the epitome of sacredness, clarity, peace and perfection.

LIGHTWORK AFFIRMATIONS:

My body is a gift and I rejoice in it.

I honor my sacred temple.

I am a vessel of light and life.

THE LIGHTNING STRIKE

It was 2001 and I was single and free, or so it seemed. I was in graduate school, finishing the last year of my master's degree and I was offered a promotion at my job that would allow me to build a treatment program from the ground up. Things were also going well with my church activities even though I continued to struggle with my spiritual walk. During the early part of that year, I starred in a one-woman show based on the life of Billie Holiday and I was traveling with the drama ministry and getting major opportunities to perform with people that I loved. I was feeling good about the direction that my life was taking and my financial situation was stable, at least, for the moment. I felt accomplished and competent. But behind all of the doing and producing, my inner child, the little girl behind the independent grown-up, was drowning in an ocean of emotion. The wall that I had constructed to hold back the murky waters of sadness, rage and fear was weakening by the day. I still hadn't slowed down long enough to deal with the years of pain from multiple failed relationships, abortions, young motherhood, overwork and the emotional wear-and-tear on my psyche from the devastation of family addiction and violence.

The constant movement and busyness kept me, and others, from noticing the cracks and leaks in the façade that I called my life. People knew my history; I shared it openly and willingly within my circles. However, I never realized that I was wearing my story like a badge of honor. I had unconsciously developed a formula for sharing my experiences that allowed me to disengage from the emotions, justify my behaviors and shield myself from attack. I hid behind the "strong woman" persona that I had created and I became a master of avoiding and deflecting my pain. I was comfortable playing this part and I tricked myself into believing that it was real. The dark parts of me would occasionally seep out in public but the main appearances of these primal, frightened pieces would occur in my home or on stage when I was performing. My daughters often witnessed or were victims of the parts of myself that I kept hidden from the public. They saw and heard my rage and they experienced my emotional numbness. I rarely hugged them or engaged in intimate moments with them. They watched as I poured my heart and soul into the ministry and my profession but they were denied the physical affection and access to their mom that others received. Both my daughters were greatly impacted by this but they responded to it in different ways. My eldest daughter adopted a defensive posture and approached the world with suspicion and distrust. She was also extremely outspoken and wanted me, her father and the world to know that she could not be controlled. She was charismatic, quick-witted and artistically gifted and she attracted a lot of attention but her rigidness affected her ability to fully express herself on an emotional level or to experience her fullest potential artistically. My younger daughter hid inside of her silence and pretended that all was well. She allowed herself to be dominated by me and her sister. We would speak for her and overpower her with our energy, thoughts and agenda. This impacted her confidence and gave her a view of the world that was steeped in fear and distrust. She was loving, intuitive, artistically gifted and had great compassion for others, but she was also passive and hesitant which sometimes attracted people who were domineering and predatory.

As stated earlier, I would remove the mask when I was on stage. I would play the roles that I was assigned and my wounded parts would come up to the surface as I brought the characters to life. I could be and do anything when I was in character and I let myself lean into the parts so that I could experience the purge. I would scream, cry, curse and spew venom when I was performing and would literally be applauded for doing it. Acting came naturally because it allowed me to turn myself inside out so that people could see what lay beneath the surface. The wailing, the cynicism, the crooked smiles, outstretched arms and raised fists of the raped, abandoned, mistreated, sadistic, angry and abused women that I played on stage were the parts of myself that had experienced the same or similar in my own life. My tears, combined with the tears of these characters, created the space for healing even when I was not fully conscious of it.

One of the principle roles that I played on stage and in my "real" life was of a fiercely independent, no-nonsense woman who told it like it was. This was a role that was very familiar to me and allowed me to tap into what I thought was masculine power and energy. The story that I created during childhood and the images that I saw throughout my life had me programmed to believe that men wielded all of the power; that they dictated how things went, and could attain what they wanted by force. I wanted to have power. I wanted to protect myself and the people that I cared about. I wanted to call the shots and to have influence over people so that they would do what I said. Taking on a masculine persona seemed like the logical thing for me to do to create what I wanted, and so I did. I was masterful at it or at least I thought that I was. On a subconscious level, I believed that I had to do this for my survival. I took on these roles in my life because I felt safe in them. I created them to keep from being devoured by the hidden agenda and abuse that I believed lurked around every corner, behind every closed door and deep within the eyes and hearts of so-called friends and family. I wore the armor and hid behind walls that I constructed to keep people from discovering my vulnerabilities and taking advantage of me, but I ended up becoming the very thing that I wanted to avoid.

While this posture served me well as I navigated school and my professional life, it did not produce the same benefits in my personal life. My fierce independence and perfectionism kept me from asking for help when I needed it. My intense drive, aggressiveness and intensity was intimidating to people, especially men. In intimate partnerships, my unspoken position was "I can do it myself" or "I'll get you before you get me." This led me to attract partners that would assist me with bringing these dynamics to life in the relationship. I manifested the things that I swore I didn't want. My mates either allowed me to control the relationships or they battled me for power and control. While the war strategy was different in every union, the outcomes were the same: battle scars and loss of light and life. Consequently, this way of being and doing would take a toll on the partnership which meant that an ending, and a bad one at that, was imminent. What usually began as an energetic, fun, passionate and reciprocal connection would end in a chaotic, confusing and/or hostile finale. Unbeknownst to me, these endings were playing out exactly the way I had designed them in my head and heart. The little girl inside of me took center stage in my relationships. She reminded me about the past when I tried to put it away. She told me that men were unsafe and that "we" were not worthy and I believed her and acted accordingly. She had control of the role and the outcomes and I let her run the show. I believed that she knew how best to manage the pain and fear that dwelled within me because she had done so for years.

So before the dust settled from the breakup of my seven-year relationship, I jumped right back into the mix again. I invited the energies of new and old men from my past to enter my life and I didn't give myself a chance to process or release the energy from the last relationship. As a result, I reactivated the old formula

AGAIN. *I told myself that I wanted to date different people to avoid unnecessary attachments and drama; however, the people that I was seeing had complicated twists and turns in their lives that mimicked relationships and experiences that I had had before. They brought the messiness of love triangles, abusive childhoods, father loss, misogyny and low self-esteem into my space and I fed on it all. I unconsciously sought to fix them as I fixed myself and was oblivious about my need to feel needed. I engaged in these relationships that had no real future or potential for sustainability because they fed the darker part of me and kept the drama that I knew so well, alive. I found myself doing and tolerating things that disturbed me, but they weren't disturbing enough to pump the breaks or bring things to a halt.*

And so, just as my cycles and patterns predicted, I started focusing my energy and full attention on one of the men that I was seeing. I had known him for several years so it seemed safe enough. He was part of my church family. We were leaders in the same ministry and he was a teacher and mentor for me and my children. I had never thought of him in a romantic way until he approached me. He simply wasn't on my radar for a variety of reasons, one of which was that he was in a relationship. However, when he started the pursuit, I responded in kind. After we secretly got involved, things moved very quickly. We traveled with the ministry together, performed and hung out. Our conversations were deep and intense, but there was an undercurrent of energy that didn't sit well with me. I couldn't put my finger on it but I knew that there was something there. I remember feeling intuitively that the connection was imbalanced but when I talked about it with friends, they kept pushing me to move forward because of who he was. I ignored the whispers that rumbled both inside and outside of me and went ahead anyway. The voices and the red flags kept going off throughout the courtship and we even stopped seeing each other several times. After a few months, the voice of the little girl who was starved for attention and thirsty for a distraction, urged me on, and he and I connected again.

There was a lot of outside energy swirling around this union. Many people were supportive, while others were shocked, disappointed and/or upset about the shady way that the relationship came about. My eldest daughter was one of the people who was hurt as she felt that I had crossed a line by getting involved with one of her teachers. She was angry because the relationship was another thing that was keeping me from focusing on her needs. She felt protective because she didn't want him to treat me like she had witnessed him treating other women in our circle and she verbalized her thoughts and stated that our relationship was a source of embarrassment for her. While I heard and understood her concerns, I did not listen or take heed. Once again, I was determined to have what I thought would legitimize who I was and the pull for that was greater than my children's wishes. This created a chasm in my relationship with my eldest daughter which grew in size and intensity as each day passed. She began to seek attention outside of the home and to shut down at school; all of which slipped by me because I was too busy constructing an illusion and chasing the dream that the wounded little girl inside of me so desperately wanted.

There were also a lot of unresolved issues due to the rebound that I was experiencing from my last relationship and all of the others that preceded it. This left a lot of things incomplete and created a slew of raw emotions and loose ends that were always energetically present even when it wasn't being discussed. This caused a major strain between us which followed us from the beginning of the partnership to the end. In addition to the more obvious challenges, there were distinct vibratory and personality differences that we were both aware of and triggered by, but chose to ignore or deny. My independence was viewed as a rejection of who he was as man while his free spirit was unnerving to me and seen as dangerous and out of control. My insecurities about my physical appearance and his insecurities about his worth showed up as overcompensation on both sides; mine appeared in the form of work and intellectual pursuits and his was in his interactions with women and his work. There was just too much baggage between us for anything solid to be established and maintained.

This was another period in my life when my spiritual gifts were resurfacing and Spirit was transmitting messages. I received multiple signs, nudges and indicators that things between us were not going to go well and that I should rethink my decision and leave the relationship to avoid being hurt and causing hurt. I would have vivid dreams where I would see him doing things that did not align with a committed relationship. There were times when we were together and I would experience tightness in the pit of my stomach that was accompanied by intense feelings of fear. I would also hear prompts or voices to check in or reflect on something that he said or did. It was all confusing and overwhelming and while I didn't completely ignore the messages, I didn't utilize the information to help me navigate the relationship and we both paid the price for that.

In the beginning of the relationship, there were many powerful experiences between us that kept the attraction alive and growing. We were both fiercely committed to our artistry and shared similar entrepreneurial goals and visions for our growth as leaders in the world. While we were together, we both grew as people, as artists and as spiritual beings and we experienced an expansion in our self-expression. We were committed to helping each other make things happen and that we did. It was also during this time that my best friend and I designed and launched our organization, Spirit of a Woman (S.O.W.), and he assisted with the development and execution of that vision. S.O.W. provided a platform for me to support women and girls as they moved from one phase of life to another and as I did the work and guided the process, it unearthed things about myself and my past that I had either kept hidden, forgotten or denied. As I worked with the girls and families of S.O.W., my inner child was being nurtured and my children, who were participants in the program, were able to grow alongside me. However, my role as Co-Founder & Co-Director, kept me in the space of "leader" and "facilitator" which did not allow me to fully experience the healing that others in the process did. Additionally, the role created a greater need for me to look and sound good which contributed to me overextending myself, overcompensating, and staying in unhealthy situations too long.

As time moved forward in the relationship, I started to question his integrity both out loud and in my heart. I wondered whether he was being honest about his intentions for me and my children. In retrospect I realize that, I, too, was the one holding back and pretending for fear that my true self would be revealed and I would be judged and abandoned. This fear based belief pre-dated my relationship with him and, thus, was part of a self-fulfilling prophesy. There were times when we were together and I would experience flashes or premonitions or hear my internal voice urging me to dig deeper into the things that he said or did. When this would occur, I felt guilty and overwhelmed by the feelings of distrust and I would hesitate before taking action. However, the few times that I followed my instincts, I discovered hidden things about him; particularly his involvement with other women and I would experience both confirmation and devastation at the same time.

This dynamic activated thoughts and emotions that were unnerving and anxiety-provoking. It unearthed feelings of paranoia, insecurity, distrust and anger that were already within me but were amplified when we were together. The feelings were so intense and the voices were so overwhelming that I surrendered to their pull and I began to slowly unravel under the power of them. My response to his behaviors and his to mine created what seemed like a never-ending wave of low vibrational exchanges. He would make a move and I would counter. I would make a move and he would counter. The dance that we were doing was out of sync and imbalanced but we kept it going and growing. These issues were compounded by my poor housekeeping skills, my low self-esteem, my flights of rage, my verbal outbursts, my attempts to use intellect to dominate him, my emotional intensity and my denial of affection and intimacy; all of which were wearing him out. I, in turn, experienced his moodiness, his judgment, his insecurities, his aloofness, his roving eye, his restlessness, his self-absorption, his wandering spirit and his dishonesty as a personal affront against me; all which kept me angry and on edge. We both started to "see" things in one another that we didn't understand or like. I felt powerless as the union slowly but surely unraveled. We sought spiritual counseling from someone that we both knew and trusted. Some major revelations about our emotional states, our pasts and our defense mechanisms came forth as a result of the work. However, there was so much pain, denial, deception and masking in the relationship that things would shift for a while and then the same destructive patterns would resurface. The arguing, lack of intimacy and sexual exchange as well as the emotional distancing continued. Just as things were coming to a head and the end was near, I discovered that we were pregnant.

When I got the news, my mental and emotional programming immediately kicked into gear and I started making decisions based on appearances and fantasy instead of reality. I didn't want to have another baby at 36 years old but I also didn't want to terminate another pregnancy or to raise a child in two separate households like I had done with my daughters. When I shared the news with him, it was clear that he wasn't thrilled either, but we made the commitment to move forward, plan and prepare for the child and continue our relationship. We threw ourselves into the planning and got lost in the good feeling of new life and a new beginning. The energy and focus that we had around the impending birth of our son was powerful and inspiring and we agreed to build a nest egg to prepare for his coming.

We both maintained our commitment and the entire family was part of the preparation. Early in the pregnancy, I experienced another layer of disappointment and devastation that I tried to dismiss for the sake of appearances and my own sanity. During the first trimester we asked our immediate family and friends not to tell anyone that we were expecting until we knew that it was a viable pregnancy. We also wanted to make sure that we were settled and that we had a solid plan for the new addition before sharing it with the community. After that agreement was made, I went away on a spiritual retreat and while I was there, a family friend told me that she knew that I was pregnant. I asked her how she knew and she said that my mate's former girlfriend told her. She went on to say that his former girlfriend contacted her because she needed someone to talk to because she was devastated after he told her the news. When I received this information, I was flooded by waves of embarrassment and hurt and the feeling of yet another betrayal. As new life was growing in my body, I felt like the energy was also being drained out of me. My best friend was at the retreat and she encouraged me to use this time to focus and care for myself. I tried to follow her advice but I was preoccupied with what I was told and spent the rest of that weekend obsessing over the situation. When I finally called him to share what I was told and to ask if it was true, I was hurt again when he admitted that he told her and justified his actions by saying that he did it to protect her. I was dumbfounded as I listened to him say that he didn't want her to be hurt and minimized the agreement we had made.

The familiar energies of anger and resentment were ignited but I quickly numbed myself and tucked them away. I didn't have time to be angry. I didn't have the courage to take a stand nor did I have the strength or the presence of mind to leave. I was pregnant and my fear about what my children, my church family and my biological family would think if I had yet another failed relationship and a baby was heavy on my mind and my heart. I also had the young women, the families and leadership team of my organization watching me and I wanted desperately to maintain the image of a powerful, responsible and balanced woman and leader. I found myself hiding in plain sight when I interacted with them as I was carrying shame about the relationship and wearing a smile on the outside while on the inside I wanted to scream. Instead of screaming, I sucked it up and I kept it moving, backwards and in slow motion.

As I proceeded to dismiss, ignore and plug up the holes that were causing spiritual and emotional hemorrhaging in many parts of my life, I was simultaneously able to immerse myself in the hope that only new life can create. There was great joy around the impending arrival of our son and positive energy being generated from our family and spiritual community. We shared every aspect of the plan together. We went to the doctor's appointments and did research. We shopped for the items that he would need and planned a community ritual to prepare for his birth. My daughters were included in everything and it felt good.

However, there was still distance and a lack of intimacy between us. I found every excuse to avoid sexual contact and since I was working three jobs—one full and two part-time—it wasn't difficult to pull off. On one hand, I felt the strong connection and energetic support about the baby and the pregnancy; on the other hand, I felt distant and disengaged from the relationship and a profound sense of distrust. As I made excuse after excuse about why I was unable to meet his needs, he grew more resentful and aloof which created an even larger chasm between us. His behaviors were a trigger for me and mine were for him and when we got upset, we reverted back to the habitual responses and patterns that were familiar to both of us. I felt a profound sense of failure as things were unfolding; however, I could do nothing to turn back the hands of time. I had hoped that things would be different when I entered this relationship, but what I thought I had dealt with and buried from my past was still alive and in full effect. Nothing had changed for me but the characters and the scenes. The themes remained the same.

The birthing experience for our son was a magnificent ritual that I will remember for the rest of my life. My mate, my daughters, the midwife and three young people that we mentored and loved, coached us through the labor and my son arrived in a safe, loving and joyful environment. Unfortunately, the weeks that followed his birth were not congruent with his entry. Within days of his birth, I became sick with the flu and was losing so much blood from giving birth that I was anemic. To add insult to injury, the baby did not latch on properly while breastfeeding, which led to excruciating pain and bleeding each time I attempted to nurse him. The first week after his birth, the entire family stayed at my mate's home and this, in my opinion, was the final nail in the coffin of our union. I remember the fitful sleep, the dreams that I had and the overwhelming feeling of doom. I tried to blame it on the sickness and post-partum depression, but this definitively felt different. There was a quiet disdain that surrounded his aura when he interacted with me. I was physically and emotionally weak and there was nothing in his vibration that was inviting or nurturing. He loved and cared for his son and did what a doting father would do, but I knew with every ounce of my being that the connection with me was non-existent and what was left landed like hot lava on a spirit that was too fragile and defeated to react.

At the end of that week I reconciled in my mind that once I went home, I would not return to his apartment again. Something in that mental declaration set things in motion for me and slowly but surely, what was left of the relationship started to erode. There were several things that happened over the course of the first year of my son's life that allowed the inevitable to manifest. All of them were part of a series of events that opened and shut the door on the relationship. Before the baby was six months old, he had to be taken to the emergency room three times and was hospitalized twice for a respiratory condition and febrile seizures. This was incredibly stressful and emotionally draining on everyone and it generated fear about the baby's health and his future. Most of these events took place during the holidays or as the family was preparing for performances. We received a lot of support; however, tension and fear were always hovering in the atmosphere.

During the Resurrection season (Easter) of 2005, I received a call that rocked my world. I was at a Good Friday service and my son's father called me to say that there was an urgent matter that he wanted to discuss with me. My stomach was in a knot as I left the service and called him back. It was then that he let me know that he had a brief sexual encounter with someone and was now concerned about his and my health and well-being. I was speechless, especially when he shared the details. As I listened to him, I felt myself sinking deeper into a dark place, but, once again, all I could think about was appearances. Yes, I screamed, I cursed, I threatened and I insulted him, but I stayed. I stayed to save face. I stayed because the prospect of being alone again was too much to bear. I stayed to show my community and family that I could maintain a relationship and a family. Even when my daughters shared that they had overhead the angry exchanges and knew the details about what had transpired, I still held on to the idea that I needed to forgive and move forward for the baby's sake. I lied to myself. I blamed myself for what happened and then when that was too much, I placed all the blame on him. I made excuses for both of us and blocked out anything that interfered with what I wanted to believe.

My staying was perfunctory. I was a shell of a person taking minimal action to address what was swirling around inside of me and I didn't want to take responsibility for my circumstances. I remember vividly what started to happen as the Creator began to move things on my behalf. The months leading up to the day that I actually took action were intense. Things were erupting all over the place and I felt scared and overwhelmed by all of the movement. I discovered that my eldest daughter was sexually active, cutting school and failing her senior year of high school and I didn't have a clue. Instead of taking responsibility for the part I played in it, I blamed her for everything and projected my anger about everything unto her. I also tried to swoop in to fix a situation that had been building for a couple of years. Needless to say, my efforts were misguided and futile. I had increased responsibility at work and was feeling pressure to lead when I didn't have the energy to think. I was building a name for my organization with my best friend and dealing with all of the complexities of working with youth and families. I was also performing on a regular basis as part of church ministry and trying to manage the intensity and demands of my leadership roles. I was drowning and the person pulling me under was me.

I was experiencing waking and sleeping dreams that were revealing the covert things that were going on around me. I was a raw nerve and the energy in my household was heavy with sadness, anger and disappointment. My daughters were in the thick of it all and were in a lot of pain but I felt too depressed to deal with it. However, in December of 2005 things came to a head. On Christmas Eve, my daughter and I, who were both a bundle of raw, angry nerves, had a huge blow up in our home that lead to a physical altercation leaving physical and emotional scars for both of us. That same evening was the watch night service at our church and the entire family attended, worshipped and interacted with the community like nothing had happened. I felt defeated by all that was occurring and the fight tipped the scales for me. After the incident, she and I mutually agreed that she would move to Virginia to live with her father once the school year was officially over and that she would finish her senior year with him. Once the decision was made, we started preparing for her move with the support of family and friends. By this time, both of my daughters were disappointed and hurt by my actions and inactions and had both shut down in their own way. My younger daughter continued to hold her emotions in silence and watched as the relationship with her mother and sister unraveled before her eyes.

This was only the beginning of the season that ignited the total transformation of my life. Less than a week after the altercation with my daughter, my son's father and I attended a Kwanzaa celebration with the baby. During the event, I had an uneasy feeling in the pit of my stomach that I recognized instantly. I had ignored it so many times in the past and this time I tuned into it, determined not to incur another loss of my dignity or power in the relationship. While we moved around talking to people at the event, my stomach got tighter as Spirit urged me to pay attention and take action. I waited for clarity but when none came, I tried to relax and put the sensation out of my head. My cell phone had died and I needed to call my daughter to check in so I asked to use his phone. It was an innocent request. I had no intention on checking his phone or invading his privacy. However, as soon as I opened the phone I saw the log of missed, received and initiated calls and among those numbers was the name of his former girlfriend listed several times; with dates and timeframes that were beyond just quick check-ins or casual conversation. After I saw the log, the knot in my stomach subsided and was quickly replaced by a dull ache in my heart but I didn't say a word. I made my call, returned his phone and sat through the rest of the event, staring ahead, as if in a trance, thinking about what I was going to do next. I was terrified, but I knew that I had no other choice. That evening he dropped me and the baby home and I spent the rest of the night thinking about a plan. The next day, I called him on the phone to end the relationship. I shared what I discovered and expressed that I had had enough.

I felt numb but I also had a deep desire to exact revenge. I shared what I believed to be valid concerns about my age, my status in this season of my life and what my expectations were regarding our partnership as parents. I reminded him that when we had our son, I had no intentions to raise him outside of the structure of a committed, monogamous partnership. I then demanded that he take his son and raise him himself. I felt trapped and, powerless, and was desperate for a way out that wouldn't leave me feeling wounded. I was also using my son as a pawn to assert my power over his dad and the situation. He said that he would take our son and we started making the arrangements but I quickly realized that my request had come from a place of manipulation and defeat so I immediately recanted it. I had no idea that my behaviors were connected to the story that I had invented as a child. I was determined not to be like my mother and the other women in my family who had been left with multiple children to raise, no relationship and minimal resources. This story, with many others lived in my head and kept me from dealing with myself and taking responsibility for all of the choices that I made and the energy that I had attracted.

After a couple of months of feeling overwhelmed, I started second guessing myself and my decision to end the relationship. I was so caught up in the story about not failing at another relationship or as a parent that I ignored every ounce of intuition that I had by requesting a meeting about a possible reconciliation. In my attempt to make things work, I asked if we could have a meeting with a few of our closest friends so that they could mediate a conversation between us. He agreed to meet and we all gathered at a friend's house to talk about what I believed would be the future of our relationship. I vividly recall the heavy energy in the room as the meeting unfolded at my friends' kitchen table. I was still dealing with untreated depression and the impact of his words, his posture and vibration took me deeper into the abyss. I remember thinking and feeling how cold, unfeeling and checked out he was at the meeting and I knew in my spirit that he showed up that way because he had already started another relationship.

When asked directly, he vehemently denied that he was in a relationship. He maintained this position even when all evidence pointed to the contrary. I didn't respond well when bits and pieces of the truth were revealed to my daughters, friends and extended family members or when I saw or heard things that made it impossible to deny the truth. But instead of utilizing the information to support me with letting go of the fantasy and accepting the reality, I insisted on keeping the drama going by confronting him about what I heard and witnessed. This did not go well and my efforts to force him to admit the truth were met with anger, lies, and pushback. It was an insane cycle that fueled one embarrassing moment after another and, all the while, I maintained the posture of the victim. The entire experience was a huge wake-up call and my resistance to the truth about myself and the situation only prolonged the unrest and imbalance that I and everyone around me were being subjected to. Consequently, my denial of the reality of my situation and the refusal to release my low vibrational thoughts and emotions had a ripple effect on my friendships, my business and my children which contaminated my environment and prevented me from finding and/or co-creating peace.

As layer after layer of my life was being peeled back, I was still trying to fix and control things. I moved forward with the plan for my daughter to relocate to Virginia and live with her father and I planned a community ritual to send her off with God's covering. Her departure was both a source of sadness and relief because she was one of the few people who could see through my façade and who would confront me on my stuff. It was my hope that the move would create new opportunities for her and that she would make up her final semester of high school in Virginia and then attend college in the south. Unfortunately things did not go as planned and the move actually triggered the revelation of a secret that my daughter had been harboring for several years.

Within the first month of her stay, I received a frantic call from her in the middle of the night. When I picked up the phone, she was on the other end screaming and crying. When she finally calmed down, she told me that she wanted to come back home because the son of her father's girlfriend had come to stay at the house and she was uncomfortable with him being there. I don't know if it was the content of what she was sharing or her delivery, but I was having a hard time comprehending anything that she was saying. However, after a few minutes of tuning in and asking questions, everything became crystal clear. That night she told me that she had been molested by her father's girlfriend's son one summer while she and her sister were visiting them in Virginia. She said that she woke up from her sleep one night and he was on top of her and that she never told anyone for fear that she would be blamed for what happened. She went on to say that his presence in the house, his comments and disrespect had triggered anger, fear and anxiety in her. She confronted him about what he did to her and told her father and his girlfriend the details about what happened which resulted in a verbal altercation and the authorities being called. Both she and I cried as she shared the story and how hurt she was about the family's reaction. That night I listened and consoled her, supported her as best I could and took immediate action to bring her back home. She and her dad stayed at a hotel while things were worked out and within a few days, one of my closest friends and her husband drove to Virginia to pick her up and bring her back to New York. By this time, my emotional tank was full to the brim and overflowing. I felt like I had failed as a mother and that history was repeating itself. All of the things I had been fighting to prevent and control were showing up in my life and I was being forced to face them whether I wanted to or not.

It was the Fall of 2006 when something deep inside of me broke and the dam that was holding back three decades of pain erupted, causing a deluge of toxicity to pour from me that I thought was never going to stop. The jig was up and the time for exposure had come. In the past, I would have been able to repair the cracks, stop the overflow and save face but this was too huge to fix. My emotions were bursting from every crevice and it took every ounce of power that I had to summon up enough energy to go back and forth to work each day. Work had always been my escape, my distraction and the proof that I was still viable and valid. I would arrive at the job in the morning, attend meetings, make calls, create strategies and supervise projects while my insides were churning from the weight of my personal life. Some days were better than others and on the bad days, I would have to hide in an empty conference room while I sobbed uncontrollably. When each day was done, I would pick up the baby, drive home and then collapse into a puddle of stagnant flesh and bones. On the days when I had to meet with my son's father for a drop off or pick up of my son or the car that we shared, I would be triggered by the exchanges and experience a set-back. Some days the interactions were peaceful and went over without a hitch, while others were tense and/or volatile.

It was all too much for me at that time. I could barely eat or sleep, and when I did fall asleep, it would only be for two or three hours before my eyes popped open and I would be flooded with thoughts and emotions about my life and the running story that I had about the great injustice that had been done to me and my children. I wanted to exact revenge and I spent hours thinking about what I could do to inflict pain and make him pay for what he had done. I was letting the negative energy overtake my mind and my ego was very much running the show. While I didn't act on the majority of my thoughts, thinking them was taking a toll on my psyche. I was turning into another person; someone and something that I didn't recognize. My saving grace was the fact that the thought of further embarrassment and the possibility of people thinking that I was weak and out of control, kept me from totally giving myself over to my rage. I also had earth angels that were keeping me grounded; friends, who would call to check on me, pray for me or meet up with me to make sure that the part of me that was rational, responsible and introspective wasn't dead.

No sleep, dark thoughts, work, childcare and sleep became my daily ritual for several months and only my daughters and a few close friends knew what I was going through. I stopped attending church. I stopped praying and I stopped listening for the voice of God. I was angry at God and detached from Spirit and the world and I didn't realize how my emotional state was impacting others around me. Just like I had as a child, I was unconsciously sending out energy, vibrations and distress calls to the world and, despite me, those signals were causing things to happen. I knew that I wasn't alone when one night I woke up from my sleep, got dressed and had to talk myself out of acting impulsively. At the same time that I was engaged in this internal debate, one of my closest friends and spiritual teachers called me on the phone and said that he had awoken from his sleep and was lead to reach out because he could feel the heaviness of my energy in his heart. That night, all I could do was cry as he prayed for me and offered me solace. I knew then that I had to do something to shift this energy or I would explode or implode; either one would be fatal.

After several months, the waters that were spilling from my soul began to slow down long enough for me to breathe and I recognized that something had to give. Just before my 38th birthday, the energy started to move and I could feel again. I was a therapist who was drowning in my own depression and my intellectual awareness and past experience with the condition helped to pull me out of the state of mind and spirit that I was in. I didn't know exactly what to do, but I knew that if things continued as they were, I would eventually be consumed.

LIGHT REVELATION

Sometimes, the MISERY unveils the MYSTERY that Produces the MAJESTY that is our DESTINY.

CHAPTER 6

"Breaking the Dam"

Sometime ago in history, eons before our births or the births of our foremothers and forefathers, we forgot who we truly were. Somewhere across time and space, we relinquished the knowledge of our TRUE selves and we began to dwell in a state of self-imposed amnesia. We allowed the deeper "knowing" of ourselves to seep out of our spirits and through our pores, leaving emptiness in its place. The chasm that once held our power, our creativity, our light and our love was quickly filled with energies of a lower vibration: fear, doubt, self-loathing and distrust of ourselves and humanity. This new paradigm and way of being was conceived, carried, and pushed out and we began to nurture it like an offspring.

We held and suckled it like a newborn babe and coddled this entity as if it were our own; ignoring its dense dark extremities, its rancid smell and its overwhelming neediness. We allowed it to feed on our spirits and it grew and thrived like any offspring given attention, a voice, an opportunity to take up time and space. When it cried out for us and called our names, we responded as any attentive parent would. We held it close and bonded with it. As we allowed its dark spirit to merge with our light, a symbiosis occurred and our spiritual antennae were lowered. We were exposed and contaminated by the pathogens of our own creation. After the bonding was complete, we became acclimated and our senses were dulled as we adopted the darkness and gave it our name and our inheritance. As each new generation emerged, the parasitic presence of our dark creation grew and became more complex, as did the amnesia. We forgot and forgot again, and the forgetting grew bigger in size, scope, magnitude and power. We were lost and we didn't even know it so we did not seek a guide, map or a compass. We were oblivious to our state of being and with eyes wide shut; we dwelled in a miasma of confusion. We forgot that our brothers and sisters were our partners. We forgot that we were birthed for co-creation. We forgot that we were spirits having a human experience and we allowed our flesh to define our fate and our fortune. When the last bit of forgetting took place and we were entrenched in this new construct, the architect that lives within each of us began to create the plans and structure for a masterful design of self-protection and survival.

The darkness that we had conceived and birthed, no longer needed us for sustenance. It was now nurturing and feeding itself and, as we sleep-walked through time and space, this low vibrational energy took root and spread. While the new energy and paradigm was unfamiliar and unsettling for us, it was also powerful, hypnotic and had great appeal. Its flow and feel was different than what we were accustomed to and the new rhythms and experiences that it generated provided stimulation and outcomes that were both provocative and addictive. This allowed us to experience new sights and sounds but simultaneously created dissonance that fueled the manifestation of fear, doubt, mistrust and the illusion of scarcity. With these vibrations circling in the air, we were propelled into a perpetual cycle of reactivity where our fear response was constantly being triggered and the need for survival overshadowed our knowledge of balance and peace.

There was now a need for survival where there had not been before, coupled with the belief that we had to fight for or against things. We forgot that we had the ability and the authority to call forth love, to activate choice, and to produce connectivity and balance at will. The presence of fear bred the fallacy of separateness and hence, the "we" that had always been our natural way of existing became "I" and the "us" that kept us aligned as a collective energy and consciousness, became "them." As we moved from being collective minded to separate minded, the possibility of rivalry, rejection and abandonment became our reality and the concept of danger took permanent residence in our hearts and spirits. Being the masterful creators that we are, our focus on danger led to the manifestation of anxiety provoking and life threatening events that reinforced our fear and fueled the cycle of cause, effect and, subsequently, suffering of all kinds.

With these energies now injected into our psyches, we developed a need to protect ourselves from all that there was and all that there wasn't. Along with the need for protection, came the necessity to create things to shield us against attack and/or annihilation by the real and perceived threats that we encountered. Both the threats and the defenses that we conjured up crossed all realms; the physical, the emotional, the mental and the spiritual. In the physical realm we created wars; in the mental realm we created nightmares and a storage space for traumatic memories; in the spiritual realm we created fear of death and in the emotional realm we created sadness, grief and despair. Every realm and dimension was colored with layer after layer of corresponding low vibrational energy and experiences and we learned to respond and react to them over and over again.

In the realm of emotion, which I am choosing to focus on because of the content of this book and my personal struggle with this realm, we designed intricate webs of feeling states with varying vibrations and levels of intensity. This made it difficult for us to understand or manage what was happening in a given moment or how to respond or react. Unlike the physical realm where we could raise our fists to ***fight*** or run and take ***flight*** when we encountered threats, our emotional responses and reactions were challenging to navigate, understand and address. Because of our lack of familiarity with the darker emotions, and our inability to control the ebbs and flows, we developed ways to try and circumvent them. The effort that we put in and the strategies that we employed were myriad and as distinct as the number of beings on the planet. We created innumerable ways to allay, avoid, deny and block the emotions so that we didn't have to deal with them but this only produced suffering in other forms. One of the subconscious maneuvers that aided us in keeping our emotions at bay was the building of energetic walls; fortresses to fend off the discomfort of dark emotions. Although invisible to the eye, the walls that we constructed had a similar or worse impact than the walls built in the physical realm and while their function was to keep negative content and experience from getting in, they also prevented light energy from getting in as well.

So we became master builders who constructed walls to dam up our feelings. We built our dams on the foundation of our entrenched beliefs and the bricks, stones and mortar that we used to build them were made from the ingredients of fear, distrust and delusion. Every brick, stone and all that held the walls together consisted of the compilation of our skewed and imbalanced interpretations of the experiences that we forgot that we created. Erecting these walls reinforced our attachment to our victimhood and our potential to be victimized and generation after generation were conditioned to believe and to operate from these paradigms.

Our dams were sturdy and dependable. They were built to last and their energy was transferrable. They could contain the miniscule feelings, thoughts, desires and memories of a single soul as well as the voluminous emotional content of an entire culture. Supply and demand were high as generation after generation sought to escape what we believed we could not control. However, we failed to realize that the more we focused our attention and intentions on managing these energies, the more they morphed and manifested into other forms. So we dug in, put on the heavy boots and resolved in our minds that the construction work would never end for our lives would continue to be filled with unhappiness, despair, disappointments, threats and near-misses; all of which we needed to be protected from. We lay the bricks, we spread the mortar, and we dammed up the deep, dark waters of negative messages, bruised spirits, lost hopes, squashed dreams, blame, shame, hurt, painful endings, and rage. We kept building. We kept damming up the waters and as they pressed against the walls of our hearts, we felt the heaviness and the pressure and we added more bricks.

Beloved, it is time for us to release the pressure; to deconstruct the dam, to drop the bricks, and to halt the construction so that we can reclaim the "knowledge" that has always been within our reach. The walls of our dams are blocking our light, our vision and our opportunity for balance and completeness. As we chose to lay your bricks and our burdens down and allow ourselves to move in the direction of feeling and healing, the haze will be lifted from our spiritual eyes and the physical, mental, spiritual and emotional dis-eases that we have been harboring will begin to heal.

As we surrender to the process and let the walls collapse, the waters (emotions) that we have been suppressing for so long will flow freely and we will experience a freedom like nothing that we have experienced before. As we allow the dark waters to touch and even sting us, over time with the application of tools that we can and will discover we will begin to wade through and swim to shore.

We will remember that the waters are ours; created by the lakes, rivers and oceans of the lives that we have lived. The waters are ours to be transformed into testimonies of triumph and as we allow the process to run its course, the fear of annihilation will slowly disappear; the force of the waves will subside and the waters will recede so that we can create anew.

LESSONS FROM THE LIGHT:

1. When we release the belief that the wall of fear that we have constructed around us has power, it will immediately crumble at our feet and light and life will emerge from the ruins.
2. There is no need for walls when our waters are flowing in the direction of love.
3. Healing waters are fluid and infinite, so let it go and let it flow.

VISIONS OF ILLUMINATION:

Greetings, Light Walker. As you take in the power of the message that you have summoned into your energetic space, I invite you to relax the parts of your body that may be resisting the greatness that is within you. Feel those spaces in your flesh that may be tense or sore in this moment. Be present to them and breathe healing energies into them so that the block can be replaced by a pathway of balanced and free-flowing energy. Breathe and release old paradigms, patterns and cycles from your muscle memory. See them floating away as your higher self-commands them to, and thank them for the role that they have played on your journey. As you clear your mind, body and spirit of these energies that no longer serve you, remember to leave space for the awesome power of the collective consciousness to support you as you reconnect to the natural rhythm and flow that existed when you were fashioned in your mother's womb. Breathe, Beloved, allow air to flow into your nostrils and hold it in your body to add life and vibrancy to the areas that need to be revitalized. When you exhale, let it represent your energetic agreement with the Universe to accept the authentic and enduring power of your greatness. Breathe and with your mind's eye, see yourself standing in your power, with your back straight and tall. Envision yourself walking on legs as strong as oak, down a winding road made of the dark, rich soil of your life's history. Feel the penetrating effervescence of the earth beneath your bare feet as you walk in the direction of your evolution. With each step, you feel the energy building in your body and your pace quickens as you anticipate what is to come. As you make your way, you can see the tracks of multiple footprints facing both directions. This road has been traveled many times and in your mind, you wonder by whom. You allow the thought to fade as you move ahead and your breath catches in your throat as you round a curve on the path and encounter a wall so massive that you cannot see above or around it. There is no doorway, archway, window or opening to be seen. There is only the wall, erected by hundreds of thousands of bricks, towering above you with the last few feet of roadway disappearing underneath. As your eyes scan the top of the wall and move to the bottom, you notice the pathway of compacted dirt and crushed blades of grass that are leading up to the wall. As you look upon the makeshift road, you notice thousands of footprints. As you make your way down the pathway, your feet slip into the indentations on the ground and you notice that many of the prints are the exact length and width of your own feet; some are smaller. As you look down at the dirt, what is revealed to you is that every single one of these prints is yours. Over the course of your life, from childhood to the present moment, you have walked this pathway, approached the wall where you've piled brick after brick to keep your memories, emotions and experiences contained. As you look up at the wall that YOU have constructed, allow yourself to recognize your own power, your own creative energy, your own ability to build and fashion with the hands that the Creator has given you. As you step on the soil of your own history, acknowledge and thank yourself for protecting yourself. As you look upon this massive edifice that you have built, become present to the fact that if you release this wall and allow the waters to come forth, the gateway for your life and new creations will be activated. Beloved, as you breathe and stand before the wall, take a deep breath and with every ounce of strength that you can call forth, begin knocking it down. Take a breath and punch. Take a breath and poke. Take a breath and kick. Take a breath and stare it down. Take a breath and shout it down. Use the magnificent power of your intention and the high vibration of your commitment to healing and transformation to deconstruct that wall. And as you engage in the act of dismantling the bricks of fear, shame, blame, pain, projection and powerlessness, watch them crumble at your feet. Beloved, you are invincible. You are unstoppable. You are the force to be reckoned with full command over your life because the Creator has ordained it so. As you watch the wall come tumbling down, step over the debris and into the glorious light of your new and transformed life.

LIGHTWORK AFFIRMATIONS:

I am free, enlightened and alive.

Love covers me. Love lives in me. I am love.

There is nothing to fear. I am safe.

A LIGHT AT THE END OF THE TUNNEL

I recall the series of incidents that led to a flicker of light shining through the darkness that had encased my life and almost snuffed out my existence. I remember wondering how my body could still be moving when I felt like I had barely enough energy to keep my heart beating. I was too frightened to bring what was happening to me to anyone's attention because I felt that sharing it would snuff out the breath that I had left. My reawakening started one day as I sat in the passenger's seat of a friend's car. We were talking and I was going through the routine of pretending like I had it together. I figured she knew something about the breakup with my son's father, but the voice of shame that was booming inside of my head told me to be quiet and to move through the time with her with my armor securely wrapped around my heart.

We were together for a couple of hours and I was feeling an overwhelming urge to escape her presence. I wanted to be home where I could hide out and wallow in my pain but the Universe had another plan. After she and I ate and talked for a while, she drove me home. Before I rushed out of the car, a piece of paper in the pocket of the passenger door caught my eye. Something compelled me to place my hand on the paper and pull it out of the pocket and when I did, I saw that it was a brochure for a clinic. The name of the clinic leaped off the page and my heart started beating rapidly as I stared at it. I sat in the car holding the brochure with my mouth hanging open. In that moment, I felt like the oxygen that I thought would never return to was now moving in my veins and reactivating my cells. The name on the brochure was "Sankofa Center for Health & Healing" and both that and the symbol below the name were very familiar to me. The image on the brochure was of a bird looking back over its shoulder with an egg in its beak. It was an Adinkra symbol from West African culture that meant "go back and fetch it." I knew it well because of the spiritual work that I had done at St. Paul Community Baptist Church and it represented the importance of learning from the past.

Before I knew it, I could hear my voice through ears that had been muffled just minutes before. I heard myself asking my friend questions in rapid fire about the center. She seemed to not notice the urgency in my voice. She just answered the questions as I soaked in every word. She shared about the center and her experience with the owner/director. She talked about the location of the office and how warm and inviting she felt the environment was. She also shared that the energy of the staff was different than other healing spaces that she had been to. Although she had shared only a few details about the center, something deep within me was firing off signals that said that this was the place where I could share myself and my pain. I had no explanation for how I felt. I just KNEW that I would get the support that I needed at the Sankofa Center and I was determined to go there immediately to get it.

As Spirit would have it, she gave me the brochure. I took it quickly, thanked her and said goodbye with new energy and a sense of hope. When I got inside the house, I immediately opened the brochure and dialed the number. I didn't look at the time or think about what day of the week it was. I just knew that I had to make the call immediately. My heart was jumping out of my chest as the phone rang and I heard the voice of a woman on the other end of the phone. It was an answering machine but I didn't care. I had gotten through. I left a detailed message with my name and number and asked that someone contact me as soon as possible. The simple act of leaving a message on the message machine gave me a huge feeling of relief. Once again, Spirit was guiding me toward what I needed to restore my life to balance and this time I was determined to grab the lifeline. The simple act of dialing the number set something in motion that I had no intention of stopping or blocking; and so my healing began.

The next day, I received a call from the owner and clinical director of the Sankofa Center for Health & Healing, Dr. Adwoa Akhu. She had a sweet, inviting voice which I recognized immediately from the recording on the center's answering machine. During the call, she asked me a series of questions and we talked about why I was seeking treatment. I remember feeling a sense of peace as I conversed with her so when she offered to set up an assessment appointment, I was elated. My appointment took place within days of our initial conversation and the experience was everything that my friend shared and ten times more. The center was located in a brownstone in Bedford Stuyvesant, Brooklyn so it had a homey feel instead of a sterile blandness that some mental health spaces have. When I arrived, I rang the bell and Dr. Akhu opened the door and greeted me with a beautiful smile. I was surprised to discover that she was a young, vibrant woman, with a small physical frame and locs like mine. She wore African garb and her locs were in a high bun. This was a pleasant and unexpected gift because she looked like so many women from the church that I had grown to love, admire and respect. Seeing her was a tremendous relief, but what I experienced when I followed her through the doorway into the center totally blew me away. The center was every bit of a healing space. When I crossed the threshold, the smell and sound of the space hit me directly in the core of my heart. There was the smell of burning incense and African music with drums and singing was playing in the background. Every inch of the space was covered with Afrocentric artwork and ethnic pieces, from masks to paintings and symbols.

The walls were painted with beautiful, warm colors and there were plants and symbols of nature that added to the ambiance that created a powerful feeling of warmth and safety. I knew at first glance that I was home and that I wanted to do my healing work in that space, with that woman.

I remember sinking into the leather chair in the room where I had my first session with Dr. Akhu. I allowed myself to exhale for the first time in over two years as I shared the reasons why I had sought counseling. I felt her acceptance of me on a visceral level, and a loving and compassionate energy was filling the space as we spoke. It didn't matter what I told her. It didn't matter that I was a trained therapist or a business owner. It didn't matter how well I spoke, how smart I was or wasn't, or how much I cried. I didn't have to hold it together. I didn't have to put on airs. All I had to do was "be" and she joined me in that place. I gave up the self-judgment that I had about my history with men. I released the resistance that I had about telling the ugly parts of my story. I simply surrendered to the process and let her hold the space for me as I purged and released the toxins from my mind, body and spirit. And so, my healing journey began in a brownstone in the heart of Brooklyn on a fall day, a week after my 38th birthday.

I was so depleted by the time I started therapy with Dr. Akhu that it took a couple of months before I gained enough strength to share the details of my life and my story so that I could get to the root of the issues and experience the revelations that would support my healing process. I was depressed and experiencing fatigue from not sleeping and eating properly. I had the additional stressors related to caring for three children, working a full-time job, running a business and recovering from a breakup. As I surrendered to the therapeutic process, I discovered that Dr. Akhu was a clinical psychologist who utilized an African-centered model to support people of color with finding their own pathway to healing. She also had an eclectic approach to treatment that combined spirituality and universal principles as a foundation for the work. During our sessions, I could talk about my experiences with my family, my race, culture, spiritual beliefs and practices, sexuality and philosophical beliefs. There was no subject that was off-limits, which made it easy for me to open up. More importantly, I discovered that she was open to talking about my spiritual gifts and intuition and how they showed up in my life. Working with her helped to ground me as more and more of these insights and revelations were unveiled. The exercises that she gave me, both inside and outside of treatment, revealed things that I had hidden from myself for decades. They also helped me to release the self-deprecating thoughts and feelings that I was harboring and allowed me to explore their origins and impact. As I got more comfortable and grounded in the therapeutic environment, I asked if I could bring my daughters in for counseling and they started their process with another clinician at the center.

Shortly after I started therapy, a serendipitous chain of events occurred that ignited a shift in my life and world view. My son's childcare provider became ill and was no longer able to keep him. I was concerned about who would replace her because he had been in the same environment since he was a newborn and he loved her dearly. As I was thinking about a course of action, I remembered that a friend of mine had opened a family daycare in her home. I had not spoken to her in a while and was feeling the heaviness of my shame about the demise of my relationship with my son's father, so I was a bit hesitant. However, I knew how much she loved children and I had trusted her with my daughters so I put pride aside and reached out. When I contacted her, she was delighted to care for my son and she had the space to accommodate our need. My son started going to the daycare immediately after and our friendship and interactions were reignited. While I had been making some progress in therapy, I was still in a space of mental, emotional and spiritual drain and disconnection and I had no desire to be social. It was the end of a rough year and I was still going through the motions; having just enough energy to perform my duties at work and doing what I had to do to care for my family. I had started attending church again and was not getting much from the services, nor was I feeling strong enough to leave the environment because too much had already shifted in my life and the community was familiar and comfortable.

My friend and her family had left the same church that I attended a couple of years before and I knew that they had started studying and engaged in non-traditional spiritual practices. Every day when I would go to the house to pick up my son, she and her daughters would share their beliefs with me and I would listen to their points and sometimes share my thoughts. I was nervous about some of the things that they were telling me because it didn't align with what I had been taught about God and religion. They spoke about the feminine aspect of God, intuition, and our power to manifest things in our world via meditation and focused energy. Although I felt apprehensive and skeptical during the discussions, I listened and absorbed what they shared with a healthy curiosity. I was also acutely aware that something had shifted in my faith and that what had moved me spiritually in the past was no longer inspiring me. This created a tremendous feeling of guilt and shame that I did not feel comfortable sharing with anyone but Dr. Akhu.

My family and I started spending more time with my friend and her family and as each day passed, I began to tune in to what they were teaching. I started studying belly dance and attending classes with her and her daughters and as I engaged in the act of using the muscles of my belly and my womb, something started to stir within me and a new found power emerged. I felt myself reawakening and tapping into a part of myself that had been dormant since I was a little girl. I recognized how closed I was as far as my sensuality was concerned and blocked in the expression of my womanhood. Through my relationship with the family, I learned more about eating live foods and taking care of my body and I found myself doing research about the correlation between healthy foods and spirituality. I read books about feminine divinity and the power of the womb. This enlivened me and made me feel connected to God and the universe in ways that I had never felt before. I was also introduced by the family and Dr. Akhu to the movie **The Secret***, a film consisting of a series of interviews about the power of the Law of Attraction and how we can manifest the desires of our hearts and achieve specific outcomes by concentrating our thoughts, energies and intentions. This concept inspired me because I had spent much of my life thinking that power existed outside of me and that it was something that had to be given to me by someone or something.*

Finally, the family exposed me and my daughters to several teachers who gave us information about different spiritual disciplines and practices. We started learning about healing, the chakras, yoga, guided meditation, channeling, the study and worship of the divine feminine and intuitive gifts. These new experiences reactivated my memories from childhood when I had intuitive dreams and would pick up on the energies of others without understanding why. The more that I engaged in meditation and yoga, the more sensitive I became to my surroundings and the people in them. The more I studied eastern philosophy and spiritual principles, the more I understood how the energy in my body worked and how to hone in on it so that I could heal myself. While I was learning and healing, my daughters were as well. They started going to counseling at Sankofa center and the energy of our household started to slowly shift as we all discovered and embraced our own individual and collective power.

My new teachers affirmed how powerful I was and talked to me about the many untapped or underutilized gifts that I possessed that were waiting to be activated. They referred to me as a healer, a title I had never even considered before, and said that my work in the world was intended to be a blessing to others. As I took in all of these new energies and ideas, I literally felt myself shifting. The darkness that had been smothering and overshadowing me for so many years was now being lifted, and a beautiful light was emerging. I was healing myself and the higher vibration that was emerging from me was guiding me toward the people and things that were making me stronger day by day.

LIGHT REVELATION

When we live by default, life is a series of crash landings, false starts and bad endings. When we live by Divine design, life is a symphony of great epiphanies, endless possibilities and groundbreaking discoveries. Discover your inner architect and start creating.

CHAPTER 7

"In Search of Higher Ground"

As we navigate the various circles and systems that make up our individual and collective worlds, we consciously and unconsciously adopt and maintain certain postures or vibrations. Every millisecond, we are vigorously engaged in the release of energetic cues to the universe that are generated by our thoughts, emotions, and life forces and activate specific outcomes in our lives. Whether we are aware of it or not, everything that we contemplate, express, act on and react to is a manifestation of our innate ability to co-create with the universe. We, Beloved, are divine architects and, as such, we have the power, the ability and the authority to transform our current states of being to bring forth something new and invigorating in our lives.

Some of us are actively engaged in the intentional exercise of divine co-creation; others are oblivious and even indifferent to it. Whether it is by default or by design, everyday that we engage in acts or rituals that go against our patterns and paradigms, it ignites a shift in our current reality. Yours may be a quest for additional resources, money or material goods, while someone else may be in pursuit of power and prestige. There are those who may desire improved health and well-being or just the ability to get through the day without succumbing to depression or the rigors of work and other life stressors. Beloved, whatever your formula is for elevated living, you are projecting and expending energy and creating a vibration that is either moving you closer to, or away from, your soul's desire.

No matter how we package our wants and needs, the universe responds and things occur. We may never voice our desires, but our thoughts and emotions initiate action on the physical plane. Our internal and external search engines are constantly projecting, producing and manifesting in ways that are either too microscopic to track or too huge to ignore. As we send out these energetic commands to *search* and seek, they are being received and deciphered by the universe in the exact way that we transmit them. Sometimes, our transmissions are unclear, confusing and distorted. You see, Beloved, by definition, the word *search* implies that something or someone is lost, missing or incomplete; that there is a need to initiate a query to flesh out the deeper meaning of a thing for the purpose of clarity and understanding. It may also mean that the origin, purpose or whereabouts of a person, place or thing requires unearthing. When our minds, bodies and spirits are indiscriminately transmitting *search messages into the ether*, it implies that our foundation or core is not in alignment with our higher selves.

When we begin to *inner*stand and acknowledge our power to live our lives by our own design, we stop looking outside of ourselves for the answers and recognize our own God-given ability to create. We also release the stories that keep us bound to cycles and ways of being that no longer serve or support us. When we give up the illusions of our imperfection and unworthiness and see ourselves as both creations and creators, we open up a pathway that ushers us into a higher state of consciousness where we are one with ourselves and the universe.

As we restore and reactivate the power of our elevated selves and move in the direction of higher ground, we begin to ebb and flow in the world from a space of enlightenment. With a newfound clarity and heightened awareness of self and spirit, we discover that the word *search* in the spiritual realm has nothing to do with what is missing or lost. The part of the word *search* that Spirit calls to our attention is the part that is a verb; an action word; a word of movement. You see, Beloved, to search also means to explore; to delve into the deeper part of something or someone in order to gain a fuller understanding and experience. Now is the time to embrace the explorer that is in each of us. Now is the time to shed the parts of us that have searched in desperation and in vain for answers that only serve to confuse, devastate and stifle our growth.

As we embrace the elevated definitions of the spiritual concepts of *search* and *seek*, the paradigm shift will allow us to approach each new experience as an opportunity for individual and collective exploration. These opportunities provide revelations that unveil the parts of ourselves that have always been present but have been tucked away by the persona called the ego. These hidden parts need oiling and reactivation for they have been made dormant by life experiences, false beliefs, fear and deprivation. My own journey toward higher ground regenerated my power and revealed to me that there is nothing within me, or in the universe, that is imperfect or flawed. This is true for all of humanity. I discovered that there was no need for me to search for that which was always there. My greatest revelation was that all I had to do was embrace the existence of my higher self and focus my intentions on doing the things that would bring me closer to it. This action, this effort, this declaration both uplifted and expanded me.

Beloved, if we are committed to exploring higher ground, we would benefit from gaining a greater understanding of what it is and how we can prepare ourselves to step into, and live up out of, that sphere. As a healer, I have worked with men and women who were adamant about their belief that such a "place" could not exist. Their earthly experiences and attachment to logic would not allow them to see beyond the solidity of form and matter. As I worked with them, I readily and authentically declared that there was no such place as higher ground. I agreed with them, without hesitation or reservation, because I knew that higher ground, as a state of being, could not be relegated to a location or space. It is simply too expansive and complex to be a destination on a map or a plot of earth in some far-off land.

Higher ground is a realm that reverberates with joy beyond contemplation and peace that stills the most troubled parts of our hearts. To achieve this place of high vibration and elevation, we must first embrace the possibility of its existence. Beloved, I declare that higher ground is an experience; a phenomenon so deep and ethereal that describing it with words does not suffice. Before I delved into the deeper spiritual work that I was called to do, I, too, resisted its existence because my spiritual walk was hindered by fear, confusion and guilt about things that I had done in my past. I convinced myself that I could not achieve anything beyond what I had witnessed and experienced in my own religious practices so anything beyond that was inconceivable, unattainable and impossible. I also believed that what I had done in my youth rendered me ineligible to dwell in such a sacred place. These beliefs permeated my psyche and only allowed me to experience spirit from the limited lens that I invented for myself.

Well, I am here to share with you that the Creator is not the trickster that we make him out to be. The universe does not engage in baffling us so that we are unable to find the answers and a clear pathway to a transformed life. On the contrary, the Creator provides simple direction and solutions for living so that we may easily find the way to our greater selves. It is our ego selves that complicate matters and create thoughts of the impossible and fears of the insurmountable. These illusions are self-generated and keep our feet anchored firmly in place and activate fears and obstacles to keep us from truly "being" the spiritual giants that we are destined to be.

So, Beloved, this message of completion is designed for each of us to become present to, and affirm, a formula for living that will place us on the road to elevation. I share this with love, for it is the formula that restored my light after I experienced one of the darkest periods of my life. I was only able to receive it when I surrendered, woke up from the deep sleep that I was in, and accepted that it was time to do a new thing. I present this to you as a choice, not a mandate. It is an open invitation to anyone who is committed to raising their vibration and transforming their relationship with themselves and the Creator.

First, let me invite you to remove the veil that is covering your third eye; the part of your internal navigation system that allows you to see beyond the concrete into the spirit realm. Removing this self-imposed barrier will expand your spiritual understanding and your reach. To achieve this, I invite you to adopt a regimen of yoga and breath work, prayer and meditation, reading of sacred text and spiritual journaling, and authentic sharing with others so that your spiritual awareness is raised to a level where you can envision the possibility of a new world; a world beyond the one that you have co-created with the help of others. As you engage in these spiritual disciplines, you will experience a release of the perceived strongholds that keep you trapped in a perpetual cycle of mediocrity and mundane living. Through your willingness to forgive yourself and others, the activation of unconditional love and positive regard, the practice of authentic sharing and the abandonment of pseudo-power and control over people, places and things, you will tap into your innate ability to hover above the surface of your life. These rituals, and many others, will be revealed to you as you allow Spirit to speak to you and through you and as you do this work you will be moved ever so gently toward your true self. Beloved, higher ground is your soul's salvation. Say "yes" and step closer to your destiny.

LESSONS FROM THE LIGHT:

1. Higher ground can be reached when we dare to tap into the deeper parts of ourselves, embrace our own humanity and the humanity of those who are our own Divine reflections.
2. The key to unlocking the door of your higher mind is to dare to believe that such a space exists and that you are worthy of dwelling there.
3. Your elevated vision provides pure, unadulterated clarity that perpetuates your highest good and the highest good of all.

VISIONS OF ILLUMINATION:

Greetings Light-Walker, I invite you to still yourself; to listen to the sounds that dwell within you and feel the delicate energy that moves around you. Listen and flow with the natural rhythms that existed before the invention of modern mechanisms that keep time, project sound and generate movement. Slow down, inhale, exhale, and in this moment, use the gift of air and ether to allow your internal systems to re-calibrate themselves. Tune in to the vibration of your own body and the power of your beingness for the Creator has given you all that you need to heal, release and restore yourself. As you feel the ebb and flow of your internal music, remember that the illusion of disharmony and brokenness was created by your own imagination and vision. Beloved, as you experience your breath, relinquish the "unnatural" inclination to measure and weigh your value by way of your perceived accomplishments. Expel from your cellular memory the desire to relish in the fallacies of lack and scarcity; of success and failure; of illusions that we've created to bring us comfort but fail to bring us closer to our highest good. So as you create sacred space around you and within you, visualize yourself standing on the top of a mountain peak. Feel the warm, gentle winds caressing your face and envision the pristine clouds swirling about your head. Call the winds to you and command them to cover you with nurturing energy as you take deep, life-giving and sustaining breaths into your lungs. Stand in your power and slowly lift your hands above your head. Feel yourself being lifted toward the heavens by the omnipresent power of the universe and experience the essence of higher living, higher loving and higher being. Beloved, your search is over; the higher ground you seek dwells deep within.

LIGHTWORK AFFIRMATIONS:

I walk in the light of my authentic and elevated self.

I AM the peace. I AM the way. I AM the One.

My path is clear and my spirit is willing.

RISE AND SHINE

It was now 2007 and my awakening from the deep, self-induced sleep that I had been in since my youth was both abrupt and exhilarating. I found myself in a constant state of euphoria. I could hear, feel and experience things on a deeper level and my heart was open in a way that I could not remember experiencing before. Every day that I engaged in the deliberate act of exploring life, I was reintroduced to a part of myself that I had killed off. All of the things that I was terrified to give up were falling away like old skin and everything in my life was up for re-examination and replacement. I no longer trusted that the life that I was living was based on my real wants and desires. I was looking at everything through a new lens and I was both inspired and scared as hell at what I saw. However, the inspiration was far more magnetic than the fear so I kept diving deeper and unveiling. I had an awareness of my body that had not been there prior. I knew that I was alive, not because of my heartbeat, the rise and fall of my chest or my ability to take air into my lungs. The aliveness that I felt was tingly and reactivated because of every other living thing that was around me. I reveled in the sensations of my body and the amplified way that my five senses were communicating to me and through me. As I continued to go to therapy with Dr. Akhu, I found that our conversations had shifted from the "woe is me" stories to declarations about igniting my spiritual gifts and the newfound power that I was discovering as I acknowledged and utilized them. I was more confident and present in my relationships with people and I felt myself connecting with them in ways that had previously been unnerving and intrusive to me. I felt an upsurge of power in my speech and my writing and I found that people were listening and responding to me in ways that they had not before.

It was a period of rapid growth for me where I invited a myriad of different experiences into my life; jumping head, heart and Spirit first into things with the support of the universe and like-minded people in my corner. I made the decision to transition from the church and the ministry that I had been a part of for fifteen years. I started studying feminine divinity with my friend and her family full-time and I joined the spiritual community that they founded and contributed to the development of the group's spiritual practice. I read and listened to everything that I could get my hands on about eastern philosophy, meta-physics and spiritual transformation. I asked for guidance from Spirit as I incorporated the information that I was learning in the group with what I was learning independently and with the synergy of all of this knowledge, I developed a series of morning rituals of prayer, meditation, yoga, divination and journal writing that I executed every morning from 5:00am to 6:00am. This was something that I never would have dreamed that I could do prior to my awakening because I had convinced myself that I was a "night person" who had an aversion to early rising. At the job, I felt a sense of calmness that brought a different energy and synergy to my work. I felt compelled to bring joy to an environment where previously I had felt unfulfilled, disengaged, drained and resentful.

I also related to my work with Spirit of a Woman (S.O.W.) in a new and deeply profound way. I recognized how I had been hiding in the shadow of my best friend and business partner and how I "made up" that she was smarter, more talented and skilled than I was. I convinced myself that I could not do the work without her and, by doing so, I placed undue stress, strain and responsibility on her which diminished my power and hers. As I took ownership for these things, I was able to remove the veil from my eyes and allow myself to see her humanity and my self-absorption. I removed her from the pedestal and took myself down from the cross so that we could function as co-creators and equals in our relationship and the work. As I exercised the muscle of my voice, I found that things were shifting and the people, places and things around me were no longer responding as they did before. My relationships were transforming as I gave up old stories and operated from a posture of love, compassion and openness. While this was not easy, it provided me with opportunities to relinquish power and to trust the guidance and direction and support of my higher mind and spirit.

I was peeling back the layers of the person who I had conditioned myself to be and what I discovered was that I had underutilized gifts that I wouldn't have known existed if I hadn't removed the blockage. I started trying new things, investing in professional training and going on trips abroad. I sought out new connections and circles of friends who were part of my spiritual growth and development. I did a ritual of release given to me by Dr. Akhu around my energies with men. While I was on a cruise to Jamaica for my friend's 50th birthday celebration, I cut the chords with those energies and expressed gratitude for every man that had ever loved, left, nurtured, supported and/or violated me during the course of my life. After that ritual, I started setting boundaries with my son's father and I requested a conversation to close the chapter on the resentment and negative energy that had been circulating around us from the inception to the completion of our relationship. In that process, I also introduced a new schedule that would literally split the care and supervision of our son in half so that we were equally responsible for his physical care and well-being. All of these actions furthered the activation of my feminine power and energy while simultaneously amplifying my relationship to my intellectual and artistic gifts. Releasing the negative energies, inviting the new energies of life, and living into my space seemed to release a valve that was holding back a storehouse of ideas, innovations, creativity, life and LIVING.

LIGHT REVELATION

Life is a call to action and action is the gateway to LIFE.

When my chest is open, the pathway to my heart is clear. If I can "see" You, then I can "find" you.

CHAPTER 8

"Unmask Yourself"

One of the most significant contributors to and mechanisms for, our cognitive growth and social development as human beings is the activation of our imaginations and the experience of "playing make-believe" as children. According to Sigmund Freud and Erik Erikson, the hours that we spend dressing up in adult clothing, putting on costumes, acting out adult behaviors and roles or using objects to create scenarios, contributes to our ability to gain mastery over our fears and allows us to explore future roles that we want to experience in adulthood. As children, each time we took on a role, reenacted or spontaneously created a scenario on our own or with others, we opened a gateway for a new set of skills to emerge and a deeper understanding of self and others to materialize. Imagination and reality were synonymous as we blended our real experiences with fantasy. In the fantasy world, there was nothing that could not be created or overcome. There was an endless supply of food, clothes were abundant, and fun was inexhaustible.

In the world of make-believe, we were able to be the princess, the king, the mermaid, the wizard, the super hero, the villain, the mother, the father, the teacher, the wind, the ocean, the sun or the fog. We got to be any and everything that our minds could conjure up. In the realm of fantasy play, we were powerful, unstoppable and invincible in our capacity to construct or deconstruct as well as start and stop the action at will. In this world, a dragon's fire could not burn, an evil king could be overthrown, and a witch's spell could be shaken off as soon as the school bell rang to end recess or the street lights came on to signal us to head home. But for some of us, the troll under the bridge was our alcoholic uncle, the wicked stepmother was actually sleeping in the bed next to our father, the vampire was the bully at school who was draining our power on a daily basis, and the werewolf was our next-door neighbor who touched us inappropriately when no one was looking.

As we indulged in the joy of make-believe, we also became acquainted with the possibility of escape. We discovered that we could create an alternate reality that would allow us to remove ourselves from the people, places and things that felt unsafe. The learning curve was swift and sharp as we discovered that adults wanted to silence us and to control the content of our sharing and the volume of our voices. During this time, it was also revealed that our caregivers were fallible and that their mistakes could not be tied up in a neat little bow with the application of magic and the declaration of "The End."

Our awareness increased and so did our confusion about the contradictions of the world and human dynamics. We began to unconsciously utilize the skills that we mastered during childhood to vanquish, transform and mitigate the impact of those realities so that we could cope with and survive the rigor of day-to-day life. As the stakes in the games of life got higher, we developed more elaborate forms of pretense and unwittingly erected structures to keep them in place. As we grew older and the unpredictability of life and all of its stressors began to cover us with a transparent sheath of toxicity, we used the skills that we acquired during child's play to conform to social expectations and to acquiesce to the pressure to act in socially acceptable and adaptable ways. It was then that we fine-tuned our capacity to internalize the negative messages that we heard, to rationalize mental, spiritual and emotional abuses that we experienced, and to deny the impact that the absence of intimacy and connection in our interpersonal relationships had on us. We pretended not to smell the stench of hate and discord that permeated the institutions that were charged to teach and guide us. We found ourselves bending and contorting ourselves to fit into the small, colorless spaces that matched the ones that everyone around us was dwelling in.

As skillful artisans, we devoted our talents, our time and our attention to the business of fashioning new faces and ways of being to reinforce our sense of belonging in the world and our "mask mastery" gave us access to the roles that we were indoctrinated to pursue. We tried on different voices and choreographed our movements to ensure that what we projected outward would fit the bill. We taught ourselves how to speak, think and emote on cue, and the identities that we constructed served us well. We learned to act the part and to blend in for the purpose of survival. After all, we were conditioned from infancy by seasoned mask wearers and bearers on the how-to's of make-up application and the procurement of props to support the illusions that we were taught to believe were real. The masks were not wrong and neither were the fantasies that they upheld. On the contrary, they were purposeful, protective and productive. They did the job and they did it well. We constructed them to stand in the gap when the fragility of our inner children would not allow us to look into the darkness or to seek out the light. The masks were perfectly crafted to fit our needs and they transformed based on each condition and scenario.

There were masks of silence and shyness, masks of over-compensation, masks of savior and saint, overachiever and underachiever; masks of heroes and sheroes, masks of scapegoats and golden children, masks of victim and dominator, masks of chivalry and villainy, virgin and whore, womanizer and prude; masks of self-destruction and masks of independence and codependence.

Masks, masks and more masks that attracted and deflected, rejected and resisted, built and destroyed, cried and denied. We held fast to them and wielded their power and surrendered to their vibrations believing that the distorted reflections looking back at us in the mirror were our authentic selves. We took tests and applied for jobs with them and attracted or repelled lovers because of them, made money or lost money while sporting them, and declared war or peace while their toxicity eroded the skin underneath.

The masks were perfect creations; parasitic by nature and impeccably constructed for survival and adaptation. Slowly and meticulously, they consumed us and we freely sacrificed our flesh for the sake of "getting along." Unlike predators, these parasites only possessed the power that we allotted to them when we created them. As their hosts, we gave them free rein and full expression and then we forgot that we gave birth to them. Consequently, our offspring overpowered and devoured us in short order. Yes, we forgot that we were the designers of our own hall of mirrors and our selective amnesia kept us in the back seat of our lives, peering through the rearview mirror, too afraid to look ahead for fear that we might actually see beyond the borders of our self-generated boxes.

Beloved, your heart may be pounding against your chest as you digest these words and their implications, but all is not lost. At any moment, you can decide that the unhealthy partnerships that you have forged with your masks can transform from a condition of parasitism to a status of mutually agreed-upon symbiosis; meaning that you and the mask-wearing parts of yourself can choose to co-operate and co-exist without overshadowing or destroying one another. You might be asking yourself why anyone would elect to maintain a false part of themselves; you might be wondering how this seemingly adversarial relationship could ever co-exist in the same being. Well, the answer is quite simple. Once the light of awareness has been turned on and the presence of the masks is revealed, a part of the power that the masks previously had over you and your life is diminished. This awareness brings your thoughts and behaviors from the background to the foreground of your mind, body and spirit. In those moments of clarity, you can choose to do and be something new.

The re-making and re-shaping of our masking behavior is an incredibly liberating and restorative endeavor. As we rediscover the parts of our being that have been dormant and disengaged, we reactivate our innate ability to regenerate and integrate all aspects of ourselves so that we can experience the resurrection of our individual and collective spirits. The Bible (Ezekiel Chapter 37:1-14) speaks of the prophet Ezekiel's vision of a valley of dry bones that were brought back to life after a long period of death and decay. While the individual bones, flesh, blood and organs were literally reconstructed and brought back to life, the revival of the bones is more symbolic of the resurrection of a people, a vision and a legacy after a period of stagnation, resignation and darkness. The reawakening of the bodies and spirits offered an opportunity for those men and women to rise and begin again, armed with the power of their experience of life, death and resurrection. With this testament as fuel, every soul who stepped out of the valley into the world was equipped to inform and inspire others to fulfill the prophecy in a way that they were incapable of doing prior to their deaths.

The same can be said for the opportunity that is availed to us when we awaken from the mass coma to discover our true selves. It is not the abolishment of the masks that will provide the fertilizer for us to remain awake and aware. It is not the rejection of our false selves that will have others experience us as transformed or authentic beings. It is not the denial of the masks or the pretense that all of the remnants of their existence are gone that will inspire others to embrace a spiritual awakening and join us on our journey towards expanded enlightenment. It is quite the opposite. What will support us with remaining conscious and activated toward a higher level of living and loving is our willingness to engage in the acts of attribution and acknowledgment. As we point to and declare that our successes and our failures have been directly connected to our ability to design and give life to our masks, then others will be able to do the same. Subsequently, they will be able to envision a life where their identities are no longer running the show.

LESSONS FROM THE LIGHT:

1. Every facet of our being serves a purpose and plays a role in our mental, spiritual, physical and emotional development; even the parts that we attempt to deny or conceal.
2. Transformation does not require us to reject the masks that we wear but affords us the power to give ourselves permission to remove them and place them on the shelf.
3. A Mask-maker is the most qualified person on the planet for the position of mask-remover. If they have the power to construct the masks, then they also possess the power to deconstruct them.

VISIONS OF ILLUMINATION:

Greetings, Light-Walker, I invite you to find a quiet space where you and your higher self can connect with Spirit. Find a space where you can and will choose to be fully present in your body and can listen with your spiritual ear. When you find the space, sit or lie down and, with gentle and loving intention, select an object or point in the space on which you can focus and hold your gaze. When you have found that point and you are tuned into its vibration and your breath, use your internal voice to invite your identity or false self to silence itself for the few moments while you engage in this meditative experience. When you offer the invitation, do so with love and compassion. Release the desire to force, rush or seek the answer. Release attachment and simply allow the communication to float toward you as you engage your breath with power and purpose. Breathe; be one with the object or point of focus and tune in with your spiritual ear. Be assured that you have the capacity to listen from this higher place. Release your resistance to this fact and surrender to the idea that this higher level of communication is possible for every spirit on the planet. This includes you Beloved. Listen and breathe slowly and steadily, letting your belly fill with air and then releasing that air from your body at the same pace that you allowed it in. As you activate your lungs, breathe and find the natural rhythm of your breath. Listen to your body as you inhale and release the air. Check in with your earthly self. Listen to the sound as air enters and leaves, enters and leaves. As you realign your body with the natural flow of breath, close your eyes and give yourself permission to be present and in tune with YOU. Let the breaths speak to you. Embrace their message and these lessons with an open heart. Allow your mind to be at rest as you still yourself and listen.

It is time to allow your true "self" to speak. It is time to remove the mask and to quiet the voices of the false parts of yourself that you have been letting run the show. As you breathe gently and settle into the silence, give yourself permission to reflect without the heavy energy of blame, shame or resistance. There is no right or wrong in the breath. It does not seek to overpower you or to control you. Its only purpose and desire is that you surrender to your own power to live and love. As you become one in partnership with your breath, give yourself permission to meditate on the various voices that you allow to invade your spirit and overpower your higher being. Give yourself permission to hear how loud or soft they are; how deep or sharp they are and the pace in which they speak. Allow yourself to meditate on when each of them choose to show up and what masks they wear, you wear, to support their message. Do you hear your mother's voice or her words when you are addressing your colleagues at work? Is your father's voice or words at the forefront when you interact with friends or family? Is it the voice of your fifth grade teacher that comes out loudly and clearly when you are sharing your dreams or ideas with someone else. Breathe and meditate on how and why these voices and the masks that they wear were birthed. Have they protected you from harm? Given you the courage to speak? Helped you to get what you want from people or situations? Allowed you to express your emotions? There is a reason why the voices and the masks were created and you can choose to look at them through a loving and grateful lens. There is no right or wrong here. There is only opportunity to observe their presence and purpose and to choose to keep them, to release them or transform them. Beloved, as you listen to each of the voices and look at each of the masks, thank each one for showing up and for providing what you felt you needed based on the moment and the circumstance. Hear and see your victim's voice and its mask. Thank them for showing up. Hear and see your defensive voice and its mask. Thank them for showing up. Hear and see your angry voice and its mask. Thank them for showing up. Hear and see your know-it-all voice and its mask. Thank them for showing up. Hear and see your manipulative voice and its mask. Thank them for showing up. Let each of the sounds and faces show up and lovingly acknowledge them for what they have provided to you and for you. And as you call each of them forth, breathe and know that you can choose to hold on to any one of them or all of them if you wish or that you can release any one of them or all of them as well. It's all perfect and so are you. Continue to breathe as you move through the voices and the masks. Be with them and allow yourself to acknowledge that they are NOT you; they are only fragments of yourself based on what you believed you needed during a particular life experience or circumstance. As you allow each of them to speak and show their faces, be reminded that you can play with the volume of the voices and the picture and features of the faces. Practice amplifying, lowering, muting, erasing, photoshopping and deleting them at will. Breathe and acknowledge your power to create and destroy. You have that power, Beloved, so use it as you choose. Breathe and remember that you called them forth and you have the power to send them away. So I invite you right now to select one voice and its mask that you are ready to work on right now. Select one that you are authentically ready to transform and allow yourself to hear its message and see its face. Remember to breathe as you listen to it and look it in its eye. Check out the features of the face and hear the sound and the message that the voice is conveying, but do not get lost in them. Now, with compassion and intentionality, imagine that you have a remote control in your hand with multiple buttons that allow you to control the volume, the picture and the power. Feel it in your hand. Imagine the color of the remote and its buttons. Press each button and use your breath and your vision as you practice turning the volume up and down and clicking the buttons to adjust the picture, the contrast, the color and the power. Take your time. Play with it and gain mastery over it. You are in control. Once you feel that you have mastered the use of your remote, then I invite you to refocus your attention on the voice and the mask that you have called forth. Listen and look at them with love at the forefront of your heart and, when you are ready, choose to exercise your ability to lower, mute, adjust, shrink or turn off the sound and the picture. Remember, you can choose to turn them off and turn them back on in one motion. It is all up to you, and it is all perfect. Breathe and make your choice. Breathe and exercise your divine right to activate your power in the direction that works for you. Breathe and acquaint yourself with your ability to create. Breathe and acknowledge that you have the power to deconstruct the masks and walk in the light of your authentic self. Beloved, what will you choose?

LIGHTWORK AFFIRMATIONS:

I choose to love every facet of my being.

I resist nothing; therefore, I free everything.

I am a mask maker, a mask re-shaper
and a mask breaker.

The Fire & the Flame

Something inside of me was reignited and I was back in touch with my true self. After years of struggle and resistance, I had finally surrendered and allowed the voice of Spirit to penetrate the wall that I had built up around my heart and the flood gates opened. I could see, hear and feel anew. Everywhere I turned, there were people, places and things that would activate memories, thoughts and emotions that, just months before I would have been oblivious to. It was like a button had been pushed and new data was bypassing my head and being downloaded into my psyche. My cup was overflowing and I could not drink enough of the healing waters. I was acutely aware of myself; my hands, my hair, my feet, the air in my lungs and the rumbling of life in my chest. The knowledge of who I am as a healer and lightworker was being communicated in every conceivable way. As I embraced the concepts and the words and as I surrendered to the magnitude of the calling, more and more was revealed to me. As the vibrational shift was occurring at full throttle, I felt compelled to release the things that might obstruct my path and my view. I was awake, aware and in tune, yet there was still something lurking inside of me that I wanted to exorcise from my spirit. As I was engaging in rituals of release and restoration, all of the intra-psychic and spiritual work that I was doing did not expel the remnants of rage that lived inside of me nor did it allay the issues of low self-esteem. In fact, it seemed that the intensity of these debilitating emotions were bubbling and churning more heavily since I woke up from my self-induced stupor. The old part of me that was accustomed to the formula of "fight, flight or freeze" was wired for survival and its life force was strong, light on its feet and throwing heavy blows at my head and my heart.

At the same time that I was experiencing this tug-of-war between my higher self and my ego, I enrolled in a five-year professional program to enhance my skills as a clinician and to broaden the tools that I utilized with the adults and young people in S.O.W. The program was designed to teach a healing technique called Psychodrama which utilizes role play, reenactments and self-presentations to allow group participants to investigate life situations from the past and present. The program was far from traditional. It was designed so that everyone in the process could practice their newly acquired skills by directing and enacting our own stories and the stories of our peers. We all brought our life experiences, relationships, our thoughts, our pain, our shame, our biases and resistance to the training and put them "in action" on stage for the group to see, experience and embody. These reenactments brought the stories of group members to life so that we could gain insight and create new and adequate actions to take in the future.

My introduction to psychodrama was definitely divine intervention. The technique provided me with powerful tools to support others with navigating their past and present life experiences and to do so by combining the two things that I loved to do more than anything in the world; acting and counseling. Additionally, the study and practice of the skills learned in the training helped me to discover a pathway to healing that I didn't know was possible. The work was shifting me on a mental, emotional and a meta-physical level. Acting out my stories and having others play the roles of people from my past, present and future life was helping me to tap in and release the hidden emotions that I had buried. The work also provided me with insights about the motives, perspectives and emotions of the people that I was in relationship with. I was able to walk in their shoes and to see the world through their eyes. This new view of my relationships and experiences allowed me to forgive and release in ways that my other healing practices had not.

Not only did the psychodramatic reenactments bring my anger, disappointments, joys and hopes to the surface, they also allowed me to bring these parts of myself to life so that I could interact with them, ask questions and explore their purpose and presence. This was a magnificent gift as it gave me the opportunity to explore my internal world by giving it flesh, bones and a voice. I was able to personify, "be with", dissect and view my rage in all of its forms and facets. Since I was a child, rage had played such an integral role in my life. It fueled so much of what I had accomplished in school, on jobs and in the community. It helped me to be creative, to speak out and speak up against oppressive people and systems. Through Psychodrama, I learned that my "ego" self, the part of me that developed unhealthy attachments and wielded pseudo-power, wanted to hold on to it. My rage was a living and breathing entity and it had a life and a plan of its own. It would have been easy for me to rest on the pretense that the rage was foreign and unpleasant for me, however, my awakened self knew that this was not true. The relationship between me and my rage was symbiotic. I refer to it as "my rage" because I created it. It was hand- and heart-crafted by yours truly and I knew it well and loved what it could do when I unleashed it. I discovered and took responsibility for this as a result of the powerful medium of psychodrama.

The rage was not part of my **nature.** *I was neither conceived nor birthed with it. On the contrary, it had moved into my heart space when I was a little girl with the intentions of establishing permanent residency. My rage was a product of* **nurture;** *conditioned and designed on my own time, with my full attention* *and creativity. It had been with me so long that I could not differentiate it from me. I surrendered to it again and again and it managed the power that I fed to it masterfully. I depended on its guidance and protection and it served me well. Its presence was so impenetrable that I couldn't see through or around it. I was accustomed to it speaking for me and when I looked at my reflection in the mirror, it was IT'S face that stared back at me. Its essence and mine were intertwined which made it hard for me to see the internal and external damage that it was causing in my life.*

Part of my confusion about the function and necessity of my rage was that we co-created and produced so well together. There were concrete, measurable outcomes that gave me bragging rights on the kick-ass power and appeal of our union. It made things happen and it moved people and situations like nothing else in my life. It created connections and opportunities for me to maneuver in my career and gave me a sense of power in my intimate partnerships. It kept people from getting too close to me and it mitigated some of the hurt when I let my guard down by letting someone in. I couldn't see the rage for what it was because it served a practical and powerful purpose in my life. This increased my denial about the negative impact that it was having on my personhood and spirit and allowed me to hold on to it, to defend it and to dismiss the people who witnessed it, called me on it and demanded that I be accountable for it.

My rage ignited things. It was the fiery flame that burst forth when my internal radar perceived that there was a threat. When this happened, within an instant, the heat that dwelled within the lower parts of me would well up and burst forward and my words and actions would create an inferno. My awareness of my ability to torch people and situations at will was heightened when

I became a member of the small spiritual community that helped me to climb out of the dark place that I was in back in 2006. My connection and exposure to their beliefs and practices allowed me to gain awareness of my spiritual gifts and to adopt esoteric practices that shifted my vibration and cracked open the door to my destiny. The re-emergence of my higher self was a magnificent experience and being in the company of this magnanimous circle of people heightened my senses and my creativity. I felt powerful when I was in the circle and I knew that I was part of something much larger than myself. However, there was something about the size, configuration, intensity and intimacy of our group that triggered some old tapes and responses from my past. As I grew closer to the group and tapped into the well of knowledge and experience that was availed to me, my empathic abilities grew in strength and intensity. Every day, I discovered another facet of my gifts and I eagerly shared this with the group and the leadership. My burgeoning gifts made me acutely aware of the vibration of the collective and its individual members. It also made me sensitive to the people that I was working with at my place of employment. This was sometimes overwhelming and unnerving as I would pick up on both the covert and suppressed emotions that were circulating in the space.

During this period, my spiritual gifts were raw and untrained and the experiences that I was having were confusing. I had not yet learned how to decipher and separate my own emotional and spiritual "stuff" from other people's, and so I would be caught up in a tidal wave of thoughts, feelings and sensations when I was in their company. The experience of my hurt, pain, confusion and rage, blended with theirs created conflicts both inside and outside of my spiritual circle that were explosive and frightening for me and others. I would be triggered by things that reminded me of my past. I would also be triggered by waves of energy that I could feel coming from each member but could not explain. With all of this brewing within me, I would then act on the impulses that were part of my old programming and it would elicit negative reaction from the members. I would then react when they reacted, which generated more fear and gave fuel to the emotions that I was trying so desperately to keep in check. As the cycle replicated itself again and again, I would try to explain and defend myself. I would point out the things that I was seeing and picking up from the group members and attempt to bully them into admitting things about themselves and their pasts so that I could reconcile with the overwhelming emotions that I was carrying. At the same time, I was experiencing the same upheaval and volatility with my supervisor at my job. This caused the tensions to mount between me and the people whom I had the most interactions with. Consequently, emotions would flare up; resentment would build up and then burst. What made this more challenging to deal with was that much of what I was picking up from the people I was in conflict with had validity. However, my style of communication, posture and timing was so off-putting to them that it made it virtually impossible for them to hear or tolerate what I was saying. The passion, which was the internal flame of my spirit, was dimmed by the firestorm that was fueled by the rage that I had stored in my heart. The element of fire was at play in my life and things were heating up and reaching the boiling point. Unbeknownst to me, I was being purified and prepared for the next level of my journey. Layer after layer of my old existence was being burned away so that my true core could be unveiled and revealed. The periodic upheavals went on for almost two years until a decision was made by the two leaders of the group to ask me to step down as a member. At first, I was shocked and appalled by the request and I tried to convince them to allow me to stay so that we could work through it. Then my emotions shifted from hurt to anger and then to shame. The old story of being "damaged goods" and "unworthy of love" reared its ugly head, but because of my spiritual practice, these feelings only lasted a short while. When the emotional dust finally settled and I began to utilize the tools that I had acquired, Spirit revealed to me that it was time for me to transition from the group and that it was all divinely orchestrated. My time with them had run its course and if they had not asked me to leave, I would have remained with them past my appointed time, which was exactly one of the patterns that I had been replicating for years. I had learned what I needed to learn and seen what I needed to see. My 40th birthday and rebirthing ritual had opened another portal to my evolution and it was time for me to move forward and continue the next chapter of my journey.

LIGHT REVELATION

Our birthing experiences are never-ending. If we allow ourselves to be fully present to the gift of rebirth, we can be "carried" in the womb of the universe; we can "develop" new ways of doing and being as a result of every experience; and we can be "pushed out" into the world again and again, fully formed and ready to crawl, walk, and then, run the full course of LIFE.

CHAPTER 9

"Stop, Drop, Roll, and Get Fired Up"

When we find ourselves standing in the fiery moments of life, it is much easier to surrender than to activate a plan to address and/or prevent unnecessary devastation. Once we surrender, however, it is inevitable that we will be smothered by the heat, scorched by the flames, overtaken by the smoky haze, and consumed by the pain of our circumstances. Many of the challenges that we deal with are temporary, manageable and can be addressed by applying concrete actions if we don't allow ourselves to become obsessed, depressed and disempowered by them. Our inability to separate the issues from who we are often prevents us from fully seeing the reality of our circumstances so that we can view them objectively, approach them creatively, and identify their birth, their development and their possible solution(s). More often than we are aware of or would care to admit, the fiery episodes become the focus of our lives and the people, places and things that are most valuable to us go up in smoke. In the midst of the situation, we make excuses, we over-analyze, we rationalize and minimize. We blame ourselves for what has happened or we convince ourselves that others are to blame as the flames get bigger. We call on people who think, look and act like we do and they co-sign our madness and the smoke gets thicker. In the meantime, a tiny fire has evolved into an inferno, leaving a trail of destruction that could have been minimized or avoided altogether if we had just said or done something different.

The dynamics in these episodes can produce a darkness within us and a toxic internal and external environment where the life, light and breath is being sucked out of our lives and the lives of those around us. With decreased air supply and little to no visibility, life begins to show up as a series of traumatic events that we must react to rather than move through with clarity and intentionality. Peaceful living becomes a fantasy that others experience and we become full time firefighters; responding to the wrong alarms, wearing the wrong gear and charging full speed ahead into the blaze with no back up in sight. Heat, flames and sirens become a welcomed and expected part of our existence; drowning out our inner voices, our intuition, our emotional compasses and our innate power to just "be".

As we dwell in this constant state of emergency, our psyches become parking lots for the refuse and debris from the fires that we have either attracted, ignited and/or chosen to fight. As the fire starter and/or fighter in these scenarios, the mobility and elasticity of our minds becomes depressed and our creative juices evaporate due to this constant heightened reactive state. As we stand in these places and adopt these postures, we are unconsciously dwelling in a low vibrational space, waiting to either step into the role of the rescuer or the role of the rescued as things land, explode or implode within and around us. In these moments, we are passively responding to life rather than actively creating and controlling it. This, Beloved, becomes our existence, our script, our climax, anti-climax and unfortunately, our ending if we don't recognize and stop the cycle.

One would think that this level of relentless misery, reactivity and commotion would create a thirst for relief and a desire for freedom that would have us looking for the nearest exit sign. On the contrary, Beloved, it is quite the opposite. Our conditioning and exposure to the hypnotic properties of the flames transforms us into human, heat-seeking missiles that both consciously and unconsciously ignite fires so that we can demonstrate how masterful we are at starting, stopping and reigniting them at will. We seek and keep the heat and we marvel in our ability to do so. We show others our burn marks and we talk about our losses and our gains from the devastation so that we can keep the flames alive in between fires. As we press and rewind our fire buttons, we train others to ready themselves for the emergencies and the drama that ensues; these individuals become our partners in crime, sworn in, dubbed and ordained to help us with setting off and fueling the flames.

Beloved, pointing out the existence of your "fire pattern" will serve no purpose if I don't support you in creating an effective exit strategy, or shall I say, evacuation plan. Identifying a low vibrational cycle without providing a formula to transform it would be irresponsible of me and would, once again, add fuel to an age-old flame. Since you are engaging in the act of reading this book and you have gotten this far, I would assert that you are committed to at least exploring the possibility of healing and transformation. Since I am committed to healing and transformation for myself and others, I am compelled to share a simple antidote that was downloaded into me by Spirit to help mitigate some of the damage and support us with releasing these patterns.

When I first received the formula, it was during an early morning meditation where the soothing heat of the sun had come through my window and was gently kissing my face. Just like the sun's rays, the message came through in the form of a wave and a whisper that got progressively louder and more intense. At first, I didn't understand. I was listening with my brain and wasn't getting it. In my frustration, I squinted, frowned and tilted my head to the left and the right as I struggled to find the meaning and purpose of the words. After a few minutes of resistance, I recognized that I had been listening through the static of my ego and I released the thinking part of myself and reconnected with my breath so that I could focus on just "being" the vessel and conduit for the message. I then stilled myself, activated my breath and listened from a posture of openness. After sitting for several minutes, the message came in with volume and clarity.

When I finally got it, I laughed out loud. I laughed for a variety of reasons. I laughed because of the elementary nature of the message and I laughed because I discovered that Spirit had a sense of humor just like I did. It was a beautiful moment that I will never forget it. Beloved, are you ready for the antidote? Are you ready to engage in a treatment where the only side effects are joy, freedom and relief?

Before you commit to the treatment, it's important for you to know that the remedy that you seek is already stored in the annals of your mind. You probably learned it as early as primary school and if needed, you could recall and activate the knowledge with ease. Do you remember witnessing and/or participating in a fire safety presentation? Firefighters would come to your school to lead these training sessions. They would be all decked out in full uniform and equipped with all of the bells and whistles that command respect and authority. Their intention was to educate us about the destructive power of fire and to teach us what to do to prevent injury or death if we were ever caught in one. I can vividly recall the demonstrations that I witnessed as a child. Each of the firefighters showed up at my school dressed in their gear and outfitted with their equipment as well as their egos. I remember the command that they had over everyone as they shared directions and tips for safety with all of the students and teachers. I recall that the instructions were given with clarity and were shared and demonstrated repeatedly so that each of us could remember and execute them in case of a real fire. The firemen drilled into us that we should listen for the bell, follow the instructions given by the fire safety officers in the school, use the appropriate exit signs and to be sure not to panic as the emergency situation unfolded. I also recall the firefighters' overall demeanor as they shared the messages and instructions that would ultimately save our lives if appropriately executed.

What was most compelling and provocative to me was the part of the demonstration that addressed what actions we should take if we were ever in a situation where we found ourselves to be "on fire." I will never forget the three simple, yet powerful commands that they drilled into our heads: Stop, Drop and Roll. As they shouted the words, something inside everyone in the room heard and responded to them.

As a child, I took the words in and I could repeat and execute them on demand. However, I never understood the magnitude of these words until that day, sitting cross-legged at my altar with the sun kissing my face. I listened intently as Spirit spoke and I heard "stop, drop and roll" again and again. As the moments rolled on, the tears of understanding, innerstanding, familiarity and opportunity rolled down my cheeks. How simple, I thought. How ridiculously and beautifully simple it was. I realized in that moment that I didn't have to fight any more fires unless I wanted to, and something deep within me was released. As I sat crying at my altar, I felt the little girl that lived inside of me smiling because she was relieved that I had finally remembered the simple command. In that moment, I chose to surrender, to put down my gear, to release the tension, to take my hand off of the alarm and just "be" with the peace. These three monosyllabic, four-letter words were both a declaration and an equation for living life and I got it. I really got it. "Stop, drop and roll" was my simple formula for expansion and it would keep me on track, out of the flames, and engaged in really living my life fully and completely.

STOP! Beloved, if we are to become the vessels of love and light that we were ordained to be from birth, then we must be willing to pause and take inventory of our walk, our talk and our ways of being and doing in the world. This self-assessment will allow us to gain access to the meaning of our lives and will provide a model for others to do the same. To **STOP** is to still ourselves so that we might gain access to the voice that lives within. To **STOP** is to create a pathway for true communion with the parts of ourselves that possess the higher truths for our lives and our destinies.

Beloved, do not be misled and please release all semblance of confusion. To **STOP** does not mean that you are stagnant. **STOP** is an action word that allows for the acquisition of spiritual power. When we **STOP** for the purpose of spiritual growth and elevation, all that we are required to do is to set our intentions, make a commitment and listen for the voice of Spirit. When we are willing to do the work and we are open to trusting the process, our **STOP** will transform into the command of **GO and GROW.** As we engage in these actions, we will intentionally invite the rays of the sun to kiss our cheeks.

Once we have STOPPED, applied the brakes and halted the action, we open up a space for release. **DROP!** This is both an invitation and a command that offers us the opportunity to free up our minds, our bodies and our spirits. When we choose to **DROP**, we make room for something new to happen. When we choose to **DROP,** we free ourselves to move, to breathe, to love, to feel and to heal. When we choose to **DROP,** we unball our fists, stretch out our arms and open our hands to receive abundance in all forms and to build that which will transport us from a state of stagnation to free flow.

Perhaps, we need to **DROP** out of the races that no longer need to be run or to release ourselves and someone else from a relationship that has run its course. Maybe we need to **DROP** the masks, the old played-out stories or the pseudo-power that we think we possess because of the roles, the positions, the labels, the titles and the beliefs that we have wedded ourselves to. **DROP** them. Let them go. Let it be and move forward.

This brings us to the final ingredient; the pièce de résistance. **ROLL!** After we release the façade, the toxic energies and the fire patterns that have been running the show, we will then have the power and flexibility to identify and **ROLL** out the plan for our lives. This plan is part of the sacred blueprint that was designed before each of us was born. With this newfound relationship to our destinies and the activation of our natural power to create, we are able to think, move and produce in ways that were once foreign to us. As we **ROLL** with intentionality and focus in the direction of our purpose, the perceived obstacles, illusions of lack, scarcity, resistance and fear melt away. Our innate gift for manifestation expands and yields outcomes that stretch us beyond what we ever imagined or perceived for our lives.

Beloved, to **ROLL** is to demonstrate our capacity to do, say or be what is necessary to put out the fires in our lives and to prevent new ones from erupting. Our power to execute gives us space to request support from others, to express our deepest desires, and to reveal our darkest secrets. It opens a pathway for our voices and visions to change the trajectory of our lives and the lives of others. When we are courageous enough to **ROLL** out our plan, there is a ripple effect that spreads like a fire that does not burn. Our movement inspires, soothes and ignites action in others and our lives become the catalyst for inspiration instead of a template for mindless replication.

STOP, DROP & ROLL: a simple command, a powerful affirmation and a recipe for living that even a child can follow.

LESSONS FROM THE LIGHT

1. When you STOP the action and activate the stillness, the habitual patterns are halted and your vision can be enhanced so that you can see, reflect and regroup.
2. When you DROP what's not working, you are exhibiting deep courage and impenetrable faith which will support you with overcoming seemingly insurmountable obstacles. You are daring to release the pattern to create space to rediscover your purpose.
3. When you ROLL out the plan, you are saying "yes" to your destiny. This focused and intentional action will be the fertilizer to manifest your destiny.

VISIONS OF ILLUMINATION:

Beloved, take a moment to silence your mind, still your body and calm your spirit. If you are able, find a quiet, comfortable place to sit or lie down. Allow yourself to adjust to the space; the smells, the colors, the energy that surrounds you and become one with that energy. Invite it to partner with you as you engage in this moment of release and restoration. As you sink into the atmosphere and the stillness, give your body, mind and spirit permission to fully be at rest. Remember to breathe deep, cleansing breaths to nourish your cells. Imagine the molecules in each of those cells being nourished and revitalized by the air that you are gifting them each time that you powerfully and purposefully inhale and exhale. It is time for you to claim your power, Beloved. It is time for you to call forth all of the elemental energies to neutralize and balance out the fire so that the power within you and outside of you can be stabilized. Remember, you possess the power to generate the fire and you also possess the power to extinguish it. The flames can only consume you if you surrender to them. The fire will only overtake you if you fail to take action. It is time to call upon the elements of water, air and earth to balance the fire, tame the flames and soothe the pain that is present in your life. So now that you are in this space of co-creation, you can humbly and passionately use the power of your internal voice to call upon the element of water; water that soothes, that purges, that expresses, eliminates and transforms. Trust in its ability to move you through the fires in your life unscathed yet fully present to the lessons that these experiences will avail to you. Release any anger, resistance or fear that you may be harboring for none of these emotions align with your highest good. Give water permission to cleanse these emotions, to lift them high above your body so that they can be transformed into energy that nourishes your soul. Beloved, you are worthy of this support so allow yourself to receive and lean into it. And now as you embrace the support of the element of water and all that it has to offer, I invite you to make space for another layer of covering as you move through the challenges of life. Take in three deep cleansing breaths and on the final exhale, create room in your spirit for the magnificent element of air; air that lifts, that flows, that regenerates and clears. As you fill your lungs with air, I invite you to connect to its life-giving and life-sustaining energy. Remember that air has the power to both feed and blow out a flame and you can choose in this moment to call forth its power to extinguish the fires that may be causing burnout, upsets, eruptions or disruptions in your life right now. Breathe and know that air is holding you up and can keep you afloat while you Stop, Drop and Roll out your plan. And now Beloved, as you indulge in the combined energies of water and air, you get to reconnect with the water that makes up 90 percent of your body and the air that oxygenates every ounce of blood that is flowing through your veins. You are the embodiment of these elements. You are them and they are you so breathe and then swallow and feel their power and presence within you. But there is more layer of covering to be had, Beloved. There is one more ingredient that you can apply to move you through the moments where you feel pressured, overwhelmed and defeated. I invite you now to create yet another space for the magical presence of the element of earth; earth that grounds, earth that stabilizes, earth that produces abundance and earth that churns out life in all forms. I invite you to celebrate your skin, the flesh that encases the body that you inhabit as it is a symbol of the element of earth in its highest form. You came from the earth and to the earth you shall return. But while you are here, I invite you to choose to co-create with nature and other living beings so that your life will compliment and contribute to the universe. Breathe, swallow and experience your flesh as you surrender to the power of all of the elements. Allow them to work with you and through you. See them in everything and in everyone. Breathe, swallow and feel as you embrace them as your allies and as they assist you with neutralizing the flame. Remember that the fire is also yours to have and to hold. Breathe, swallow, feel and emote as all of the elements move around you. Remember that all is well and the universe is aligned with your success.

LIGHTWORK AFFIRMATIONS:

My life will start when I create the time to ***STOP.***

Today, I choose to **DROP** *the fight to initiate my flight.*

I possess the power to **ROLL** *out the plan.*

A LIGHTWORKER UNVEILED

At the close of my thirties, a major shift had occurred in my world. Like a phoenix, I emerged from the fire, having recovered from multiple emotional and spiritual wounds that I believed would never heal. As I approached my 40th year, the joy that emerged from my soul was palpable; its sweetness combined with my heightened awareness of spirit kept me well-nourished and energized as I prepared myself to re-connect with the world after a long period of separation. This was one of the most significant rite of passage experiences that I had ever had. The experience allowed me to remove the masks and to shed the layers of dead skin that were buried beneath. This skin had a history, a feel, an aura and an odor. It had been with me since before I could remember; hanging loosely from my body like an old cloak.

It had taken 30 plus years to reach this pivotal moment and I had finally decided to release the dead weight. After years of soul-searching, falling and rising and falling again, intense spiritual study, sacred rituals and purging, I was finally ready to declare to the world who and what I was. There were representatives from every circle that I had been a part of over the course of my life; each individual had contributed in some way to my journey and now they were gathered to witness and support what I considered to be my spiritual rebirthing. That night as I was home preparing for the gathering, I was acutely aware that my crossover from earthwork to lightwork would complete one phase of my preparatory process and would be the start of yet another phase. I knew that once the night was complete, my sacred contract with Spirit would be re-activated.

Not everyone who gathered on the evening of my 40th rebirthing ceremony understood the magnitude of what I was *doing. There were even some who would not support it if they knew. Despite this fact, I knew that their presence was a necessary part of my process and so I embraced all of the energies and I pressed forward. During the months leading up to the gathering, all of my dreams, visions, moments of meditation, messages and instructions pointed to the same conclusion. I was to stand before the community, share my story, engage in sacred rituals and declare to a room full of witnesses that the next leg of my journey had begun. I had to release something to gain something and to risk something to become something. The simplicity of this was both overwhelming and invigorating.*

My awakening had come in waves and the transformation that ensued was so powerful that it is hard to describe in words. The Spirit, in concert with my higher self, had orchestrated it that way so that I could not resist or retreat from the magnitude of the responsibility. So on a frigid night in October 2008, adorned in white and silver in honor of the sacred occasion, I crossed over from a space of earthbound resistance to a new realm of my spirit-led regeneration and the last layer of miasma that was resting over my third eye was removed. As I completed each of the rituals that were designed by the priests and priestesses in my spiritual circles, I felt the warmth of Spirit that lived within and around me increase in size and intensity. As I felt the Spirit beckoning me forward, I fully embraced the invitation from the heavens to step out on the edge of my life and take up the mantle that every lightworker is presented with when they are reminded about their sacred contract. Little did I know that some of the teachers, confidants, friends, family and supporters who had been there with me, and for me, over the years would not be in my life as my 40th year unfolded. As I embraced the call of lightworker, new doors, gifts and resources were revealed and unveiled and some of the energy of the people, places and things that I had held on to from my past were released from the box that I had imprisoned them in.

Sometimes, the journey to higher ground requires that we take an unfamiliar route through unchartered and uninhabited territory. Sometimes, the people and places that we encounter look nothing like we imagined or expected. Beloved, the path and purpose of a lightworker is not to be predictable or prescriptive. The lightworker's path is one of hills, valleys, swamplands and deserts. The path to higher ground for one called to do lightwork on the planet is driven and inspired by the needs of the masses. As we prepare ourselves for the journey, we may find ourselves standing alone on the precipice of our own awakening.

LIGHT REVELATION

There are times when the darkness of the world appears to eclipse the light that radiates from our Spirits. Beloved, do not succumb to fallacies of hopelessness or helplessness. Just like an eclipse, the darkness is temporary. When your inner glow appears to be fading due to life's challenges, remember that Spirit has emergency lighting that always illuminates the way.

CHAPTER 10

"Creation as Creator"

We are Creations, intimately tied to every element, every tree, insect, animal, and living thing on the planet and every particle in the universe. We are flesh, blood and bones with a set number of days behind us and a set number of days before us. We are intimately connected to the universe with all of the ingredients of the divine swirling in and around us. Each of our births was the manifestation of the activated energy of humanity, of love, of hate, of passion, of lust, of boredom, of violence, of malcontent, of attraction, of unity, of insanity, of spirituality and all of the biological urges and surges that come with it. A series of chemical actions and reactions triggered both the conception and the birthing process and then we arrived as tiny replicas of our forefathers and foremothers; co-created from the biological cocktail of our parents' DNA. What an exquisite design for the continuation of life.

We are also Creators, gifted architects possessing the wand and the will to craft that which can build, destroy and transform our worlds. From the fertile soil of our mental, spiritual and metabolic toolkits, we construct our lives by default, by design or a lopsided blend of both. We declare, visualize and conjure up things and our utterances call things forth, whether we are conscious of it or not. No matter what our status or level of focus, something is always being produced in real time and space. Whether we are engaged in frenetic, haphazard activities, deliberate, well-orchestrated plans or in a season of inertia where we have to check our own pulses to see if we are still alive, our capacity to create is always activated and triggering things both inside and outside of ourselves. Here, too, is another demonstration of the miraculous and ingenious formula of our human and spiritual existence.

Acting in either of these roles—creator or creation—comes with a myriad of benefits as well as challenges for human beings. We, after all, have the privilege of being a species with a brain that operates with cognitive, emotive and moral functioning as well as a "mind" that calculates, conjures, perceives and envisions things. However, even though we have the ability to think, we are not always "mindful" or conscious of our thoughts and what they produce. In fact, it is our mindlessness that has caused the short circuit and disconnection from our higher selves; the part of ourselves where our spiritual intelligence is housed and gives birth to creations that edify, balance and produce higher vibrations and outcomes in the world. Our higher minds flow without corruption by the disharmony that exists in the people, places and things around us. This elevated and spirit-centered part of ourselves helps us to regulate and filter through the low vibrational thoughts, impulses and primitive machinations that our ego-based minds produce. Being mindful, sentient and present allows us to re-member that we are creators working in concert with nature, the universe and other human beings who also possess the capacity to create from the higher mind if they so choose. This level of presence and spiritual intentionality permits us to dwell in our role as "creator" from a place of conscious, grounded energy.

With this energy as a foundation and driving force, we are able to stay connected with everything and everyone in the universe. We create rather than produce things from a state of being that is grounded in loss, pain, limitation and fear. Our higher or spiritual mind keeps us from dangling like puppets on the tenuous strings of our ego-driven, fear-based concerns and desires. This higher level of thinking, doing and acting, allows us to recognize that we are most creative when we are tuned into the network of souls that are part of the collective unconsciousness; emitting energy and intentions into the pool of ingredients that produce abundance in all forms for the greater good of everyone and everything in the universe. As we dip, drink and co-create from this well of power, what we produce will be in balance with all things. As such, the integrity of these creations will be unshakeable and impenetrable.

Now, Beloved, being present, mindful and intentional as we move in and through the roles of Creator and Creation is no easy undertaking. The level of focus and self-awareness that is required to consistently produce and harness the energy needed to keep these egos of ours in check is an exercise that calls for much practice and deep introspective work; work that most of us are unwilling to do. Imagine what it would take to juggle the thousands of thoughts that run through our minds on a daily basis, as well as tuning into our emotional ebbs and flows. Couple that with the push, pull, press and probe dynamics that we engage in with the people, places and things in our environment. Just thinking about the prospect of managing all of these provokes feelings of anxiety.

Consciously choosing to be a Creator and consciously operating from the role of Creation are revolutionary choices. Whether we choose them consciously or not, we will never cease to be them. We can never resign, quit, transfer, or renegotiate these roles. In this human form, we are the essence of all creation and the representation of the creative force. We are designed from birth to generate from these roles and we will continue to do so long after we die. Think for a moment about the chemical process that a decaying body undergoes when it ceases to generate life as we know it. The flesh breaks down, transforms and gives life and breath to other organisms. Thus, the creative energy of the creation continues to yield matter in an innovative and powerful way.

With the level of disconnect, disdain, dis-ease and debate about the essence of who we are and what we are able to do and be, it is challenging for us to relate to ourselves as awesome beings and to embrace our ability to alter matter and shift worlds. Inside of this resistance also lives an aversion to being nurtured and celebrated for the phenomenal creatures that we are. Therefore, we cannot fully be powerful, intentional and responsible for what we manifest as "creators." Without engaging in the grounding energy of spiritual disciplines, receiving the support and mentorship of enlightened teachers and guides as well as having a willingness to maintain an open channel of communication where the voice of the Divine can be heard and felt, most of us will go to our graves without ever gaining access to the miracle of our existence or the connection that we have to every living thing in the universe.

It is important to note that there are some of us who choose not to acknowledge the power that we possess in these two realms. They choose instead to remain passive with their creative energies as well as their power and limitations as creations. They are fully aware of what being in these roles can call forth and they have chosen to refrain from utilizing the energy. They are present to the fact that the synergistic effects of these two postures, when both are fully engaged, can activate a powerful blend of pleasure, pain, mental, spiritual and emotional devastation as well as outcomes that can be the catalyst for enlightenment or the igniter of results that confound us and leave us feeling like we are floating in a state of suspended animation. These outcomes can be unnerving, and for those who are afraid to go "deep," they can disrupt the script that they are living from.

While it is safe to say that most of us don't want to tap into something that might cause mental, spiritual or emotional upset, it is also important to remember that denying our natural flow and our innate connection to who we really are does more damage over time. Our inability, or blatant refusal, to tap in on this level, can block our access to balanced and harmonized living. When we resist the natural order of things and our place within that order, what ensues is the corruption or the blemishing of the psyche which also contributes to diminished, stagnant or inconsistent outcomes in every aspect of our lives. This keeps us in a constant state of spiritual and emotional conflict. The impact of the imbalance that this creates in the universe can be seen and felt everywhere.

Rejecting the role of creator means that we relinquish our power and shirk our responsibility for our actions and their impact on others. We deny, blame, neglect and project so that we don't have to take ownership for our contribution to the darkness or the light that exists in the world. We distance ourselves from our creations, and in doing so, they are left unclaimed, unattended and unloved by us. Dismissing the role of creation means that we are free-floating like feathers in the breeze, unrelated to the brilliance of our beingness and disconnected from our parts in the grander scheme of things. When we are out of touch with our value as creations, we function like our arrival on earth was a product of a science project gone wrong instead of a deliberate act of spiritual love, generosity and reciprocity.

Beloved, I invite all of us to step boldly into our power to create and to stand solidly in the love that was poured into us when we were conceived, carried and pushed out of the womb. It is only through our collective awareness, agreement and acceptance of these roles that our connection with each other and the Divine can truly be seen, felt, and experienced. As creations and creators, our purpose is to continue the cycle of life; conceiving, manifesting and giving birth to ourselves again and again so that we might access the true essence of our existence. To truly create as the Creator designed, we must be willing to see and tap into the divinity that is humankind. We are Creations and Creators. And so it is.

LESSONS FROM THE LIGHT

1. Your greatest gift to yourself and to mankind is to activate your creativity with boldness and intentionality. Creating by default means that you are ALIVE. Creating by design means that you are LIVING.
2. The greatest show on earth is a creation in motion.
3. There are people in your life who will never fulfill their purpose because you have not fulfilled yours. Your action and inaction creates a butterfly effect. Your choice to live a safe, predictable life may be preventing a newborn on the other side of the planet from fulfilling his/her destiny.

VISIONS OF ILLUMINATION:

Greetings, Light-Walker. It is time to create. As the architect of your own experience, you have ushered in this healing energy and this opportunity to shift and shape your earthly experience. Embrace your power and allow the new spiritual data to be downloaded into your psyche. Give yourself permission to walk in the light with aliveness, awareness and intention. In this right now moment which is the only moment that you truly have, I invite you to lie on your back, on a bed or on the floor. As you lie down, find your comfort and if there is anything in your space that is causing interference, make the adjustment so that you can give yourself the gift of enlightenment and spiritual restoration. As you shift your body, adjust your thoughts and align your spirit with your intentions, imagine that you are floating on a cloud of goodness where nothing but soft, cool breezes and healing energy are supporting you, surrounding you and holding you up. Allow every muscle in your body to sink into the cocoon of safe space as you absorb the sacredness of the present moment. Tune into your body and "be" present to what it is communicating to you. Notice the tense places, the tingles, the sounds, the parts that are relaxed. If there are places in your body where you feel tension or resistance, acknowledge them; thank your body for communicating with you and then give yourself permission to release them. Take your time and tune into what is happening with every part of yourself. Remember, you were created with the ability to tune in to yourself; to speak to every single part of you and identify the need. Notice those places in your head, your neck, your shoulders, arms, chest, heart, stomach, waist, genitals, legs and feet that are tense or sore and release your desire to judge or ask why. Simply allow yourself to be present to every part of your body and with compassion at the forefront of your heart, breathe healing energies into your vessel; the awesome house that shelters your spirit. Lovingly release any blocks so that balance can be restored and the gateway to your elevated self can be opened and passed through. Breathe and give yourself permission to release old, archaic cycles and paradigms from your muscle memory so that space can be left for nothingness to emerge. Breathe, Beloved. You are the creator of your own experience and you can choose to embrace peace right here and right now. Let air flow through your nostrils and hold it in your body for a few seconds so that your organs, muscles, arteries and every chemical that activates the systems is nourished and energized. Inhale and exhale as a symbol of your energetic agreement that you are the essence of greatness in the flesh and power in the spirit. Breathe, and with your mind's eye, see yourself floating above the room and looking down at your beautiful body. As you float, let your breath support you and allow the vision of yourself to expand. See the color in your face and the curve of your lips. Notice the rise and fall of your belly as you breathe and the ever so slight movements in your hands and feet.

As you dwell in this space of openness, allow the power of this revelation to wash over you and declare with every part of your being that you are one with all things. You are intricately connected to every being, every object, every element and every vibration. You are one with your body. You are one with your mind. You are one with your spirit. You are one with the birds. You are one with the trees. You are one with every living thing and they are one with you. You were created so that you can create. The existence of "I" and the existence of "It" are one and the same so let your spirit feast on the truth of this Oneness for your interconnectedness with every particle in existence is anchored in the divine, universal agreement. My throat began to open up as if something outside of myself had pressed a button and activated some untapped force in my vocal chords. As the internal rumblings continued, I watched the bird, took in the sky, felt the tenderness of the air against my face and, in that instant, I remembered. My spirit remembered; my womb remembered; and all of my internal mechanisms remembered — the truth. Beloved, you are one with everyone and everything in the universe and all is well.

LIGHTWORK AFFIRMATIONS:

I am the conductor, the orchestra and the symphony of my life.

I am a whole, complete and magnificent Creation.

I declare and manifest the desires of my heart.

CONCLUSION

We are all Light-Walkers and at any given moment, we can choose to stand in, move toward or move away from the darkness or the light. This is the gift that was given to us by the Creator and this is the power that we can yield to ensure that the lives that we live are purposeful and contribute to the forward movement, evolution and transformation of the planet. The life journey of one soul creates a ripple effect that reverberates across the universe and leaves an energetic and spiritual imprint on the planet. We are all souls in human form and we are part of the collective consciousness. Therefore, every experience, story, belief or circumstance that we have in these bodies is intimately tied to something or someone else. Because of this fact, it is important for us to walk, breathe and live powerfully, intentionally and wisely.

Beloved, now that you have read this book, you can choose to further activate your internal flame by reviewing your stories, reflecting on their impact, releasing the residue that does not serve you or others, and restoring your power and position on the planet. Your efforts, whether they be intentional or not, will ignite a shift in the world that will be experienced by all of the interconnected energies and lives that are part of your physical, mental, emotional and spiritual storyboard. You will never know all of the people, places and things that experience the effect of the shift, nor will all of the souls, entities and energies be aware that your work was the catalyst for it. On the surface, your healing experience may appear as if it only impacts you. However, your light walk journey transcends your single existence. In fact, in order for your destiny to be fulfilled, you will have to be self-less, generous, sacrificial and vulnerable with the other souls that have been placed on your path.

You will not live to see or experience the full magnitude of your light-walk journey. In fact, some of the changes that occur in the world as a result of your work may not be visible and/or measurable in the traditional sense. Many of the shifts will be on a mental, spiritual or emotional level which can be hard to concretize, itemize or correlate to one experience or another. Furthermore, much of the impact of your transformation will undoubtedly show up way after you have passed away and new generations of light-walkers are born.

That being said, it is important to know that the heart of this work is not about you or yours. The heart of the work is about the realignment of order in the universe and the restoration of our divinity as a collective body of spiritual beings. As each soul reawakens to its true self, something powerful occurs that transcends that single life. What happens is beyond the scope of this book but must be mentioned so that you will understand the power of your work and the magnitude of your worth. Your birth added an ingredient and an energy to the universe that did not exist before your spirit and your parents' DNA merged to generate the original masterpiece that is you. Without you, life would not be as it is right now and without your light being fully activated, life will not be what it can be.

This book is an invitation to recalibrate the energy that you possessed when you first entered the world. It is one of an infinite number of gateways that can and will lead you back to your truest "self" if you would only allow it. Dear one, if you are truly committed to rediscovering the light path, you must be willing to unpack the innocent, open, expressive, forgiving, shameless and blameless parts of your childlike self. It was your inner child that first revealed the light to you and showed you how to walk courageously and fervently in it, and it will be your inner child that reacquaints you with the light now that you have lost your way. Your little boy/little girl is the seeker, the guru, the breath and the salvation that already lives within you. He/she knows the value, recognizes the need and is waiting for you to give him/her permission to shine again.

ABOUT THE AUTHOR

Shawnee Renée Benton, LMSW, FDLC, is the Founder and Executive Director of The Griots' Healing Circle, a boutique consulting business offering innovative coaching, counseling and training experiences to individuals, groups and organizations seeking to expand their power, purpose and impact in the world. She is a master teacher, healer, inspirational speaker, vision coach, playwright, performance artist, psychodramatist and mother of three who has devoted her life to the service of others. Shawnee utilizes the powerful mediums of psychodrama, sociometry, energy work, sacred rites, the healing arts and storytelling to guide her partners in healing toward individual and collective transformation and catharsis. She is also the Co-Founder and Co-Director of Spirit of a Woman (S.O.W.) Leadership Development Institute; an organization devoted to transforming the lives of women and girls across the planet.

Made in United States
North Haven, CT
05 July 2024

54412204R00104